SANITY IS SEXY

MANTRAS TO INSPIRE A HEALTHY MINDSET

DIANA ANTHOLIS

SANITY IS SEXY
Mantras to Inspire a Healthy Mindset

Cover Design: Steven Antholis
svenom.com

Author Photography: Lora Warnick
lorawarnick.com

First Edition

ISBN-13: 978-0692454794
ISBN-10: 0692454799

To those who want to live their lives truly unleashed

CONTENTS

Do your thing and don't care if they like it.

– TINA FEY

INTRODUCTION

I didn't feel like myself for ten years. The real trouble started when I was in college. All of a sudden something that comes naturally to all of us, something many of us don't even think about, stopped working for me: my digestive system. All I knew is that I was comfortably eating and drinking whatever I wanted, and one day I woke up a completely different person, not able to digest anything I was attempting to fuel myself with.

I felt sick. I felt tired. I felt disgusting. I felt scared.

My favorite meals left me bed-ridden with pain. Simply thinking about a night out with friends at a restaurant left me with fear. Watching everyone else eat whatever they wanted left me in tears. My once confident, happy, smart self withered into a hole of confusion. I felt betrayed by my body, desperate to figure out why this happened to me overnight.

My roommate at the time suggested lactose-intolerance so I stopped drinking milk or eating any dairy products (seriously, pizza and ice-cream were off limits now?). I became the queen of substitutions at restaurants, the guest who had to check-in with the host earlier to find out if I could eat the food being prepared, and the person who had to eat earlier for fear that I would be able to eat nothing. You don't realize how many meals contain dairy until you cannot eat it.

I looked like a skeleton. I lost a ton of weight I didn't need to lose. Traveling was awful. I barely ate for fear that I would be sick. No one wants to be the sick person on public transportation. I'd become so paralyzed with the fear of getting sick, I was getting even sicker.

As time went on and I introduced myself to all kinds of non-dairy alternatives, I noticed that it wasn't always dairy though that made me sick. Pizza and ice-cream were off the table, literally, but salad dressings, bowls of fruit, and hamburgers were no-fly zones as well. My intestines didn't discriminate. They favored equality. It was time to bring in the professionals.

The first doctor I saw barely acknowledged me as a human being. His staff verbally assaulted me as I walked in the office only ten minutes late due to the torrential downpour outside and delayed subways. He spoke to me as if I were a little girl incapable of understanding adult words. He wondered why my blood pressure was high. Before he even got the results of the blood tests they ordered, he recommended an endoscopy and possibly a colonoscopy.

Despite his recommendation for two very invasive procedures based on absolutely zero test results, I decided to wait for the results of the blood test. They came back perfect. He gave me a prescription for some drug that was supposed to sooth my intestines and basically forgot about me.

I suffered a few more years before I visited a second gastroenterologist, a much nicer woman who was better educated. She suggested it was IBS and told me to buy a fiber supplement I could buy in Duane Reade. If that didn't work, we could do a sigmoidoscopy because I was too young for a full colonoscopy. She literally was half-assing the situation. The fiber worked though! I was completely shocked and relieved. I started to feel normal again. Until I didn't. The relief wasn't consistent but it was better than no relief.

After suffering through a couple more years, I went to a Naturopathic doctor, a physician who focuses on natural, herbal remedies. This doctor told me I had food sensitivities, including the protein casein, which is found in cow's milk. Most of the foods that came up on my food sensitivity test were completely accurate because I had symptoms with all of them: ranging from indigestion to bloating to red splotches on my chest. I tried a few of her natural supplements, probiotics, and flower oils but nothing really worked.

Throughout the years of suffering and fruitlessly seeking relief from multiple doctors, I had also transferred colleges, worked in three high-stress advertising agencies, was in and out of a few relationships, had moved across the country twice, and was trying to figure out my next step in life.

The second day of graduate school was my breaking point. I almost didn't make it to the first day of my second class that semester because I was in so much pain. I was doubled-over waiting for the metro to arrive, barely able to stand up straight. I was so nauseated I skipped a few metros to be sure I wouldn't become sick on the train. I had just entered into an intense 10-month masters degree program. Stress was about to become a daily acquaintance and I knew by then that stress only exacerbated my problems. I was determined to find a solution.

Even though stress was amplifying my discomfort, no one could really define stress for me, including myself. How does one relax, anyway, besides going on vacation? I had nothing else to go on so I ran with the food sensitivities thing. I found an expert online and started changing the way I ate food. I learned about soluble versus insoluble fiber. I ate soluble fiber foods first during my meal and saved insoluble fiber foods for last. I was careful about what I ate on an empty stomach and only drank room temperature water. I tried a recommended self-guided 100-day "hypnotherapy" program developed by a gastroenterologist in the United Kingdom, which was basically 30 minutes of meditation a day. I didn't realize that at the time because meditation wasn't a popular word then.

I still had ups and downs constantly and still didn't feel like myself. I was still nervous. I was still stressed. Only I was nervous and stressed because I was afraid I'd be sick so my stress was only multiplying.

Even though I was feeling better, I was still looking for a cure. Yoga helped. Exercise helped. Doing work I loved helped. I was getting there, but not exactly where I wanted to be. One random day a year later, the cure came to me in the form of a book: *The Mind Body Prescription*. The author, Dr. John Sarno, is known as one of the first doctors to promote the mind-body connection. His work has healed back pain for countless patients who had no or little structural damage, but still suffered from chronic pain. This particular book discussed the mind-body connection being responsible for all kinds of pain in the body. There was a short chapter on digestive problems and that's all I needed.

I immediately buried myself in research about the mind-body connection. I sought out every resource, buying programs and self-coaching. It was a miracle in the truest sense of the word. With my newfound knowledge and awareness, I had a shift in perception. I was completely in control of my mind and body. I was finally me again.

I learned that stress is an umbrella term for a wide range of thoughts and emotions, and that those thoughts and emotions, if not felt or dealt with, can manifest themselves as physical pain in the body. Every emotion is energy, and that energy needs to flow through the body to be released. Only we don't always let our emotions flow through us, we hold them in. We don't allow ourselves to feel sad, angry, hurt, embarrassed, or nervous. We hide them, because they're too painful. Our brains, responsible for this, are trying to protect us from feeling badly but it's only making the situation worse.

I dug deep and brought up feelings from the past. I kept a daily journal, writing down every single thought and feeling I was having no matter how upsetting or embarrassing. I asked myself the hard questions, the questions I had been avoiding for years. I was able to make connections from events of the past to pains of the present. By doing this, really getting in touch with and questioning my thoughts and feelings, I was able to talk myself through any physical discomfort. Any time I had the beginnings of stomach pain, I could literally ask myself questions to make it go away. Little by little, the pain started to disappear. With being mindful of the foods I was eating and mindful of the thoughts I was thinking, I started to feel like myself again.

Shortly after, I started the Unleash Your Sexy movement. I had to share my results. I had to give out the secrets. I had to help others feel confident and sexy again, because I couldn't let them go ten years like I did. It wasn't only for people with digestive troubles, it was for people with any discomfort in their bodies and their minds. Headaches, migraines, back aches, extra weight, stress, nerves, anger, sadness, disappointment, rejection, poor body image, self-doubt, lack of self-esteem, or zero self-confidence. The mind-body connection was the secret to feeling better and I knew I could help.

I took every piece of knowledge I researched and learned over the years that worked and put it into one program for clients, and a year later, my bestselling book, *Unleashed: Live the Balanced, Centered, and Sexy Life You Deserve*. My clients and readers started seeing results. They were losing weight, feeling happier and more confident, reducing stress and nerves, and having better relationships with others and themselves. They started living the lives they wanted and deserved. They became unleashed.

During my self-exploration and coaching, I used one particular technique every single day. It was a way to have a mental check-in, a direct path to my intuition (my true self), a way to snap out of whatever self-destructive, nerve-wracking, stressful thought was trying in invade my mind and body, and a way to push away the fear. **The mantra.** A short phrase or word that clears my mind and helps me focus again. A cure. A fix. A secret potion.

Every Monday, I deliver a new mantra with a story, lesson, or quote to inboxes around the world. And countless responses to Monday Mantras flood *my* inbox each week. People can't wait to read the next one. They are powerful. They have changed lives. My mantras start your new week. They allow you to let go of last week and focus on the present. They give you something new to think about, talk about, and take action on. They make you better. They keep you sane.

You want to feel better. You want to learn more about yourself. You want to feel free. You want to feel calm. You want answers.

Sanity is Sexy is a compilation of three years of my most popular mantras, plus new ones only my clients hear. They are enhanced, rewritten, and designed to be used when needed. This is your manual for living an unleashed, sexy life, to carry around with you or keep on your nightstand or coffee table. It's your elixir. It's your medicine. When you're feeling down, there's a mantra for you. When you're feeling unmotivated, there's a mantra for you. When you can't forgive someone else, there's a mantra for you. When you feel disappointed, there's a mantra for you. When you want to be more appreciative and grateful, there's a mantra for you. Refer to this book often to guide you through challenging times and lead you to your life unleashed.

Each mantra is like a mental check-in to keep you sane. It's a cure. It's an ah-ha moment. The mantras are divided into four sections: Believe, Expansion, Find Freedom, and Feel Invincible. You can search the contents for what resonates with you in that moment. You can read through the entire book and then go dive in when needed. This book is going to be your best friend, comforting you and snapping you out of your funk at the same time (while providing the advice, solutions, and action steps of a life coach who knows just how to talk to you).

Life is what we make of it. We can choose how we are going to feel every single day. Sometimes we forget that though. Sometimes we let our thoughts and emotions get the best of us. We know it's not really us, but we don't know how to snap out of it. We just want to feel better. We just want to stay sane. Sanity is sexy, so get ready to unleash your true self.

BELIEVE

HEALTH. VITALITY. SELF-FULFILLMENT. PLEASURE. HARMONY. SUCCESS.

We're searching.

Searching for the secret elixir of happiness and the abundant fountain of prosperity.

We are on a quest for the answers. We inhale quotes. We scour Internet articles. We buy stuff we don't need.

And we expect the same result every time.

Only we don't receive what we expect. We temporarily find a hint of pleasure, but we begin our search again the next day. Thirsty for a more immediate, glamorous result.

We fight ourselves every step of the way. We add more pressure to get ahead faster. And in doing this, we absorb and exude detrimental energy.

We don't realize though, that we have had the answers all along. In our minds. In our bodies. In ourselves.

You have what you want, but you sabotage yourself into thinking that you don't.

You know who you are, but you are clouded by insecurities.

You exclaim what you want, but you've lost your faith in attainment.

If you shift your perception, blow away the clouds, and restore your faith, your quest will be much easier.

Luckily, or miraculously, there are nine mantras awaiting your absorption. Each is designed to provide you with the answers to thrive.

Health. Vitality. Self-fulfillment. Pleasure. Harmony. Success. These can be yours. Soak them in.

LET IT BE EASY
YOUR MINDSET CAN CREATE MIRACLES
KNOW WHO YOU ARE
YOU ARE THE OBSERVER OF YOUR THOUGHTS
ACT ON WHAT THE UNIVERSE PRESENTS TO YOU
ACCEPT WHAT YOU CAN'T CONTROL
BE KIND TO YOURSELF
LIVE IN YOUR REALITY
LOVE WHERE YOU LIVE

LET IT BE EASY

We put exorbitant amounts of pressure on ourselves to be the best. To be ahead of the trend. To be an early adopter.

There's so much pressure.

To wear the new hairstyle of the celebrities.
To have the designer website.
To have more an epic Saturday night…and document it.
To possess the latest iPhone.
To be the perfect wife.
To have ballerina legs.
To actually enjoy eating quinoa burgers.
To namaste your way through the day.
To effortlessly melt into downward dog.
To freeze and be electric shocked in a mud race.
To secure more stamps in your passport.
To have the most expensive car, biggest diamond, drool-worthy house, prestigious job…

Why are we so hard on ourselves?
If the things on that list make you happy, then that's wonderful. If you're doing it for outside approval because that approval will make you happy, then we have another situation.

Why can't we be happy with what we have? Why can't we find the beauty in our own lives?

We complain. We want more. We don't appreciate.

What would happen if we stopped fighting ourselves? If we let things happen naturally? If we stopped thinking so darn much about it all and just lived?

What if we stopped complaining that we have no money? Because we always find the money for what we want.

What if we stopped complaining about having no time? Because we always find the time for our priorities.

What if we stopped complaining about living a better life and actually started to live it day by day?

Stop fighting yourself. Let it be easy.

Today: What can you stop fighting yourself on right now? How can you add in something you want to your life today? Appreciate your life. Don't make it complicated. Let it be easy.

YOUR MINDSET CAN CREATE MIRACLES

If you wish really hard, the miracle you ask for will come true. Right? Wrong. You may be wondering what the heck a miracle is, considering pop culture leads us to believe it's like magic. But are miracles really comparable to magic?

> *A miracle is a shift in perception from fear to love—from a belief in what is not real, to faith in that which is. That shift in perception changes everything.*
> — MARIANNE WILLIAMSON

Exchanging your anxious thoughts for peaceful ones. Believing in yourself instead of doubting yourself. Shifting the way you think can result in a miracle.

When you make this shift in your mindset, things start to happen that blow your mind. When you stop worrying about money, money comes to you in unexpected ways. When you stop thinking that you'll never get that job, relationship, or opportunity, it comes to you.

Our bodies are made of energy. When you are filled with stressful, anxious energy, it is felt by others and they may pull away from you. When you are filled with peaceful, confident energy, others are drawn to you.

Which would you rather have?

Today: Breathe. Every time you have a stressful or anxious thought that simply doesn't feel good in your body, breathe through it. Deep breaths. You don't have to get fancy, but if you want to, one of my favorites is this: Breathe in one second, hold. Breathe in another second, hold. Repeat this until you've filled up your lungs with all of the air you can. Then slowly, very slowly breathe out. Repeat this 3-10 times depending on how much you need it.

After you have breathed your way into a more centered state, ask yourself what good can come out of what is making you anxious. How can you turn a fear into love? Yes, you will be able to come up with an answer.

KNOW WHO YOU ARE

A feisty, flirtatious, beautiful woman entered an assisted-living facility at 84 years old. She was on the younger side of the median age group. She snagged a boyfriend almost immediately, a 95 year-old veteran who wouldn't take no for an answer. The other ladies in the facility weren't happy about this. They judged her and talked about her behind her back. One time they approached her, criticizing her and calling her names. She had one response.

I know who I am.

When people try to tear you down, it reflects on them, not you.

As a people-pleaser, she was bothered that these women were spreading harsh lies about her. As a confident woman who is highly aware of who she is, she said to herself, "I know who I am."

We all have strengths and weaknesses, but if we accept ourselves for who we are and step into the world knowing this, we can eliminate negative emotions that we absorb from others.

We try to be the best we can, but we are also human. We feel sad. We feel down on ourselves. We compare ourselves to others. We try to be perfect. We wish we were better. We think that everyone else is entirely whole and perfect.

But that's not true. Words or actions directed towards you by others is a reflection of their inner thoughts, insecurities, and turmoil. It has nothing to do with you. You have simply triggered someone else's experience. What makes you different from them is how you choose to present yourself to the world.

I know who I am.

We all have strengths. Focusing on them expands them.

We all have weaknesses. Focusing on them expands them.

Which do you want to grow?

Today: Think about a situation that is bringing you down or someone who is projecting their insecurities onto you, and repeat to yourself, "I know who I am." Say this aloud if someone is criticizing you to your face.

YOU ARE THE OBSERVER OF YOUR THOUGHTS

"I need this." My mind was racing as I arrived to the new yoga studio. I was invited by the owner and instructor that day to join in her class and grab a tea after.

I was new to the area, even though I had grown up there. Everything was different. I was older and felt like a big kid in a world that was supposed to be familiar, yet felt so far away.

Someone I had known my whole life was in the class. That only made it harder. I had to explain why I was there, after living in so many other places. My heart was broken. But fortunately as I started to explain what happened, she said she knew. I held back tears and settled in on my mat.

"You are the sky, everything else is just the weather." The yoga instructor softly exhaled this quote by Pema Chödrön during class. She then added, "You are the sky, the clouds are your thoughts." It felt like a bolt of lightning went through my body.

I focused on this idea of your thoughts as clouds. I visualized myself as the vast, blue sky. I watched each of my thoughts pass by.

Some thoughts flew by. Some thoughts lingered longer. Some swirled in like tornadoes. Some bit like lightning. I told myself, "Let them pass by. Don't focus on them."

Releasing your focus on the weather in your life helps you separate yourself from your thoughts. You can have over 80 thoughts about one topic. When you think that much about one thing, it's easy to get caught up in the weather. If it only rains for an afternoon, do you keep the rain for the rest of the week? Do you carry winter's ice into summer's sun?

Your thoughts form in the logical, practical left hemisphere of your brain. In general, the left hemisphere is the dominant side. It is responsible for judgement, comparison, analysis, and the dreaded "what ifs." It connects information from the past, present, and future to form stories. But are these stories true? No. Sometimes these stories are completely false. They are lies. The left hemisphere doesn't distinguish between fact and fiction.

When we believe untrue stories haphazardly pieced together by our many different thoughts, we can start to feel inadequate. We feel anxious, sad, and angry based on stories that we've made up in our minds. How does this make any sense?

You are not your thoughts, your thoughts are separate from who you actually are. When you detach yourself from each thought, you give your thoughts less weight. Especially when your thoughts are fearful, negative, or assuming.

You can choose your thoughts. You can tap into the right hemisphere of your brain to look at the big picture. It's responsible for your intuition, inner peace, love, joy, compassion, truth, vision, empathy, and living in the moment.

Choose your thoughts based on how you want to feel. Choose your thoughts based on what you want to accomplish. Choose your thoughts based on the possibilities. Choose to let the weather come and go, releasing it.

You have a choice. You can choose the clouds in your sky. Which do you choose?

Today: Are some clouds lingering longer than you would like? Are you allowing the weather to pass? Visualize yourself as the sky. Let the clouds pass by. Acknowledge them, then detach from your thoughts. Choose the thoughts you want to have.

ACT ON WHAT THE UNIVERSE PRESENTS TO YOU

The universe brings you what you want. You've heard this saying before. That you must be open to the universe and let it guide you through your life. I could have been the person you heard it from, because I'm a big fan of declaring what you want, but one key step is missing. You must act on your declaration in order for it to happen.

You can't only say, "I want to make a lot of money" or "I want a boyfriend" or "I want to travel the world" or "I want the body of a Victoria's Secret model" and expect it to simply come to you while you sit on your butt. You have to act.

The universe may present you with certain situations in your life. It may present you with a business idea, a hot date, a free vacation house in Bali, or a personal trainer. It may be dangling that opportunity in front of your face. It may bring someone new into your life. It may guide you to a place to search. But you have to do something about it.

Think about what you really want out of life right now and take a good look around. Is there something that you want lingering in your life but you don't realize it? Pay attention. Reply to the email. Meet the new person for lunch. Seize the travel special. Sign up for the new workout class. Take action and do something about it.

For example, in 2012 I decided to re-learn French after a visit to Montréal. I said to myself, "This is ridiculous, the language comes back to me when I'm around people who speak it, so just start studying again and do it!"

A few weeks later, I met my now-husband who is French and we live in Paris (as of 2015). At the time when I didn't know he would become my husband, I was thankful for someone to practice with and thought it was pretty cool that he popped into my life. I thought, "Wow, I asked for this!" Now looking back, I think the universe took my thoughts very seriously. I had also asked for a very specific man to enter my life as well. Obviously, I paid attention to my surroundings. Et voilà.

It may sound silly, or you may not believe it until it happens to you, but purposefully take a look around to see what's happening in your life that will bring you one step closer to what you want. Make deeper connections with friends and acquaintances. Talk aloud about your goals and dreams. Perhaps you already put in the work and now it's coming to fruition. It's finally paying off.

It could be right there waiting for you. Seize it.

Today: Think about what you want to ask the universe and look around to see if it's already waiting for you.

ACCEPT WHAT YOU CAN'T CONTROL

During my first year of high school, I joined the track team as a sprinter. I quickly learned distance running wasn't for me, so I usually skipped the after-school practices that involved running farther than 400 meters at a time. I was always top ranked in the races I'd actually show up for, so I didn't see the point. My coach sarcastically mentioned how great I could be if I actually came to practice. I didn't care. I only did that for one year, and instead decided to focus on my volleyball skills, a sport I really loved.

So ten years later, I decided to set a big, audacious goal for myself. I was going to run a half marathon. I thought I had lost all of my sanity.

That meant I had to start training, which meant I had to run almost every day. This was high school all over again. At first I hated it, but I remembered my goal. I pushed and pushed, until I started to enjoy each run. But one day, I felt a very bad pain in the arch of my foot. I had minor pain before, but it immediately went away with some stretching. This time, it decided to stick around.

I was angry. I was pushing myself to complete this goal. A goal that I questioned during every run but continued with out of stubbornness and determination. I wondered if it was a sign.

The pain persisted and I ultimately had to take a break from running. I followed all of the must-do procedures: bought arch support inserts, iced, rested, elevated, etc. I did cross-training, weight lifting, and yoga. But no running. I desperately wanted to get back on schedule, but I realized that I needed to rest as much as possible so I didn't injure myself further. Oh, the irony.

I had to accept that I had to take a break from training for the half marathon. This was frustrating. In that moment, I had no control over my injury. It was there, trying to tell me something. I could either listen or ignore it. I listened. I had to listen. If I didn't listen, I could have had a much worse situation.

Sometimes things you can't control get in the way of your schedule, like a sickness or an injury. Sure, there are preventative measures that you should have taken, but you didn't. Now you know better.

It's important not to beat yourself up because you are falling behind on your training, workout schedule, or work because of an injury or sickness. Your body is telling you something—you need to slow down. That's why the injury or sickness came up for you. You're going too fast. Now your body is stopping you.

Whether it is reducing excess stress in your life or as simple as buying a new pair of sneakers, you need to listen to your body. That's the mind-body connection. When you start ignoring what your body is so obviously telling you, trouble starts to happen.

Today: What are you trying to control that you can't? Accept it. Stop fighting yourself. Stop telling yourself that you'll never catch up. You'll be able to come back stronger if you take the rest you need now.

BE KIND TO YOURSELF

For 10 years, I wasn't in tune with my body. I didn't know what that meant then though. All I knew was that stress was physically affecting me. After multiple doctor visits and struggles with having my body act irregularly, I finally discovered the mind-body connection. (My full story with glorious details is in the Introduction of this book.) When digging deep to figure out why I felt so awful, I unearthed buried emotions from past experiences. Those emotions manifested themselves and made quite the home inside my body because I never dealt with them. I pushed them aside because it hurt. And who wants to hurt? I surely didn't.

Needless to say, it took me a while to figure this out. Every time I had a very stressful event happen, my body would react. But once I gained this awareness, worked hard to understand my emotions, and learned to feel them as they were occurring rather than suppressing them, I had complete control over my body. As I have written, we all have so much more control than we think.

In that moment of pain or struggle though, it's hard to believe you have control. It's hard to be kind to yourself. If your body is acting out on you, you start to shun it. You ask why this is happening to you. You don't understand why you can't just be normal like everyone else. You stand out, and not in the way you want.

Maybe backaches prevent you from exercising with your friends or playing sports with your kids. Maybe stomach aches prevent you from eating out at restaurants and enjoying meals. Maybe sciatica pain prevents you from travelling and dancing at special events. Maybe you are sick with the flu, a fever, or a sinus infection every few months and can't work or live normally with these interruptions. Maybe your weight prevents you from feeling confident and sexy.

Whatever it is, it doesn't feel like you. Every time that discomfort comes, you beat yourself up a little bit more. Every time you are mean to yourself, you only make the discomfort worse. The discomfort is a result of your emotions, feelings, and thoughts. The worse you talk to yourself, the worse the discomfort will be.

Be kind to yourself. Rest your back. Sooth your stomach. Massage your muscles. Go to sleep. Love your skin. Then ask yourself what's happening in your life that could be causing this discomfort. Are you worried? Anxious? Upset? Think about the events in your life that are emotional. Are you allowing yourself to feel those emotions? You may not think you are stressed or upset, but your body is telling you otherwise. Listen to it and ask it why it is acting like that.

Each time this happens to me, I make more progress than before. I don't ignore my emotions or push them aside. I identify all of the reasons I could be feeling out of tune with my body. I recognize every thought and feeling that is going through me. I don't allow my emotions to become stuck energy in my body, causing me a physical reaction. I am able to feel and let go. This is a huge accomplishment. I am kinder to myself and it shows.

Any time a negative thought arises about you and your body, try to catch that thought in the moment. Why aren't you being kind to yourself?

Today: Are you experiencing physical discomfort or reactions? Has it been a pattern? Think about what's happening in your life now, how you feel about it, and if certain events bring on a physical reaction. Find the pattern and bring awareness to it. If you talk negatively to yourself, try to catch yourself in the act.

LIVE IN YOUR REALITY

"You don't live in reality."

When your spouse thinks your travel plans are crazy. When your parents think that quitting your job is ridiculous. When your friends think your plan to move to another country is insane. When your in-laws don't understand your family traditions. When you just think differently than others.

Does any of this sound familiar? I suspect you have plenty of your own stories.

If you think a different way than others, they think something must be wrong with you. They wonder how you could possibly think any differently. People like to think their reality is everyone's reality.

If you want to travel the world, make that your reality. If you want to go back to school, make that your reality. If you want to change your job, make that your reality. Your reality is completely and entirely what you make it.

Don't let others tell you that you aren't being "realistic." What is realistic anyway? Is there a universal definition of reality?

No. There isn't a reality for everyone.

This happens in families, your own and the one you marry into. This happens with friends, as you grow and evolve in different directions. This happens with spouses, as you may come from different backgrounds and experiences.

Everyone wants you to think the way they do. And if you don't? You're judged. You're told to change. You're not accepted. You're not understood. You're laughed at. You're made to feel like you don't belong, that being different is a problem.

Why though? Why do others want you to be like them? They're afraid. Afraid to make a change. Afraid to live differently. Afraid to go against the status-quo. Afraid to be non-conformists. Afraid to be disappointed. Afraid to fail.

So they end up projecting their own issues, their own views, and their own experiences on you. They think that their way is the best way and the only way. And that makes sense if they weren't exposed to different ways of thinking.

You have to accept them as they are instead of fighting them. And you have to ask them to accept and respect you as you are. You can try to open their minds to new experiences and new ways of thinking, but don't expect them to change.

Next time someone says compares their reality to yours, say, "I love my reality."

Don't let it get to you. Live in your reality. Defend it.

Today: Listen for this commentary on living in reality or being realistic. For anyone who tries to change you or tell you that you aren't realistic, practice saying, "I love my reality."

LOVE WHERE YOU LIVE

Happiness comes from within. You can be happy wherever you are because it is a choice. You choose to create happiness in every decision you make and every thought you have.

But sometimes happiness comes from a place. A place that feels good. That feels like home. That feels natural. That feels like that's where you're supposed to be.

The room, the apartment, the house, the city, and the country you live in matters. The place where you live is a reflection of you. Are you being portrayed accurately?

Start with where you spend the most time. Your bed. Your desk. Your kitchen. Are those places providing you with positive energy? Do you love crawling into your luxurious, fluffy bed covers at night? Is your desk arranged comfortably and beautifully? Does your kitchen have all of the appliances you need to prepare delicious meals?

What about your apartment or house? Do you need an office area? A yoga area? A meditation area? A morning tea area? Are the colors making you feel cozy or energized?

Perhaps your space only needs to be de-cluttered or reorganized. Perhaps it needs a complete makeover. When you add to, subtract from, or organize your space, you bring in energy. In feng shui, the ancient art and science of harmonizing and balancing energy in your living space, you can organize each corner of your home with items that bring a certain energy. Colors, elements, and objects enhance your reputation, wealth, health, and romance, for example.

I use feng shui in every space I have lived in. Whenever I've reorganized or focused on a specific area of my living space, I have experienced tremendous growth for that category. As soon as I rearranged my desk and put it in the wealth corner, more money started coming in. When I redesigned my bedroom in the love and marriage corner, love ran into my life. Research it and try it on your own (it's easy) or hire an expert to come and look at your home.

Next, think about the city you live in or want to live in. Does it provide you with inspiration? Does it bring you peace? Does it feel like home? Is it filled with the energy that makes you feel alive? Do you know you're meant to be there?

Where is that place for you?

Why aren't you there?

What can you do to get there?

Asking yourself these questions can help you pinpoint the must-have desires in your life.

It may not be possible to move cities or countries right away, so start with your current home. But don't squash your dreams just yet. Ask yourself these questions to love where you live.

Today: Find inspiration. What can you do right now to dress up your living space? If you're ready to take it to the next level, what city would you love to live in?

EXPANSION

DESIRE. FORGIVENESS. ACCEPTANCE. STANDARDS. PROGRESS. EVOLUTION.

You want others to be like you. To make decisions like you. To love like you. To live like you. To change.

But they don't change. They don't act like you. They don't live like you. And when they don't, your feelings get hurt. You blame your feelings on them, as if they are causing you to have these feelings. You believe your feelings are someone else's responsibility.

They're not. You can't control the behaviors of other people. You can't control their priorities. You can't control who they are or who they become.

The only person you can control is yourself. You create your own feelings.

You also cannot control the feelings of others. You may want to so you can protect them or so you can create the outcome you want. But when you try to control others or expect them to act a certain way, you only feel disappointed. And disappointment is a feeling you can avoid.

Understand that it's not your problem. Other people are not your problem. Other people's feelings are not your problem.

Accept others the way they are. Only keep those who are serving you in your life. Say goodbye to anyone who is wasting your time or energy. Set your standards and abide by them.

Expand your mindset. Expand your perspective. Understand and take responsibility for your feelings. Focus on yourself and the way you want to feel. The rest will fall into place.

Use the next eleven mantras as your guide to expand your view of yourself and others.

ACCEPT OTHERS AS THEY ARE
FORGIVE FOR YOU
FEEL THE WAY YOU WANT TO FEEL
IT'S NOT YOUR PROBLEM
YOU CAN'T PROTECT OTHER PEOPLE'S FEELINGS
YOU DON'T HAVE TIME FOR THAT
SIDELINE THOSE WHO ARE RUINING YOUR GAME
DON'T LOWER YOUR STANDARDS
DISAPPOINTMENT DOESN'T HAVE TO EXIST
RELATIONSHIPS ARE NOT HARD
ATTRACT YOUR IDEAL RELATIONSHIP

ACCEPT OTHERS AS THEY ARE

You're waiting.

Waiting for them to do it. Take action. Say what you want them to say. Be who you want them to be. Give what you want them to give.

You're waiting for appreciation. For help. For recognition. For a response. For love.

It's not coming through. They're not like you. They don't see the world the same way you do.

Don't expect someone to give what you give.
Don't expect someone to do what you do.
Don't expect someone to spend money how you spend.
Don't expect someone to grieve how you grieve.
Don't expect someone to love how you love.
Don't expect someone to gift how you gift.
Don't expect someone to be how you are.

Having expectations for others doesn't serve you. Remember that everyone has different life experiences, which causes them to think, behave, and act differently. They don't do things the same way. It has nothing to do with you, but everything to do with them.

So instead of waiting, instead of letting it consume you, instead of allowing the inaction of others to take over your mind…start giving.

Give appreciation.
Give help.
Give recognition.
Give a response.
Give love.

We all want the same thing. We all want to be encouraged, appreciated, and loved. And if we aren't receiving what we want, we rebel and give the opposite of love. We yell, we ignore, or we insult.

Next time someone acts out, is stressed, feels down, gives attitude, cries, yells, or is mean, remember that it's not you, it's them—wanting love.

Give it to them.

When you provide this energy, when you provide others with what you want, when you provide others with what you wish you were receiving, then it will come back to you.

Be you. Give the way you give. Gift the way you gift. Love the way you love. You'll be happier being you and accepting others for the way they are.

This will change your life.

Start the trend. Don't wait for it to come to you. Give. And don't expect anything in return.

Today: Choose someone in your life today and give them all you wish they were giving you. Give love to the person who is giving you a hard time. You can close your eyes and wish them peace. Or you can send them a message giving a compliment. Do what feels right to you. Try it, and expect nothing in return.

FORGIVE FOR YOU

It can be really hard. Someone's wronged you. You are hurt. Revenge and anger are looming in your mind. You can't let it go. It's affecting your entire being.

Forgiveness. This word is thrown around like it's easy to forgive someone for something that doesn't align with your true self. For something that has seriously hurt you.

What is forgiveness? Forgiveness is changing your attitude and thoughts towards another from negative emotions to the ability to wish another well.

It's not solely something you do for the other person. That's where many people stop and refuse to understand. There is another part to forgiveness.

Forgive for you. Forgive for your inner peace. Forgive so you can live in the present instead of the past. Forgive so you can end the pattern of negative thoughts.

When you shift your mindset and tell yourself to forgive someone not for them, but for you, the game changes. You are forgiving so you can continue on with your life without judgment, anger, or sadness.

To forgive doesn't mean to forget. Do not forget, but do not constantly remember. If you completely forget, you may allow this behavior back in to your life. Not forgetting allows you to notice a pattern and eliminate it.

Forgiving another means that you are choosing to not let their actions bother you anymore. It doesn't mean that you have to stay friends with this person or be fake. This works for friendships, colleagues, and lovers. Sometimes we must forgive to continue the relationship with someone without holding a grudge. Sometimes we must forgive so we can end the relationship with someone and move on.

Forgive them, because not forgiving them causes you too much unnecessary pain. It doesn't mean you are accepting their behavior that made you angry. It means you are not letting them affect you any longer.

And what's better than that?

Today: Who do you need to forgive but can't? Hold that person in your mind. Think about how you can forgive them. Repeat, "I forgive you, for me, because it's not worth my time or energy to keep thinking about what you did. I forgive you for what you did."

FEEL THE WAY YOU WANT TO FEEL

No one can make you feel.

Only you create your feelings…based on your thoughts, your expectations, and your beliefs.

Other people may try to make you feel. To suck you into their vortex of emotions, disappointment, and frustration.

But you have the choice. You can get sucked in or you can walk away.

Think about it. Are you making decisions based on other people's feelings? The answer may be surprising. We stay friends with someone because we don't want to hurt her feelings. We agree to the restaurant choice of the group even though we hate it. We travel to a place we never wanted to see because we couldn't say no. We stop everything we're doing to be there for someone else. We even stay in relationships we don't want to be in because we are afraid to hurt the other person.

Are you making these decisions for yourself or based on how others are going to react?

Why? Why are you letting others dictate your decisions? Why are you letting others dictate your happiness? Why are you letting yourself get sucked in only to feel terrible because of someone else?

You have to stay true to you. Don't let other people's feelings control your happiness.

It's never personal. It's never about you. It's always the other person. Sometimes, someone in our lives could be feeling bad or having a rough day and it rubs off on us. Don't soak in someone else's feelings.

Focus on you, focus on how you're feeling, and focus on not letting other people's feelings become your own. Many people sacrifice their own happiness to accommodate others. Make decisions that will make you happy.

Feel the way you allow yourself to feel. If you're not feeling it, don't.

Today: Are you making decisions based on someone else's feelings? Think about a decision you recently made or need to make and ask yourself if you made that decision based on you and what you want or based on the potential reaction of someone else.

IT'S NOT YOUR PROBLEM

We can absorb the emotions of others. We feel their energy flow right into us. We become someone else's feelings, soaking them up like a sponge.

While this intuitive trait is admirable, it's exhausting. You can spend a lot of time absorbing someone else instead of yourself.

The next time you find yourself completely soaking up emotions, energy, and feelings that aren't yours, remember this:

It's not your problem.

It's someone else's problem. It's not yours to be concerned with, to take up space in your brain, or to cause you unnecessary stress.

When others are going through circumstances, problems, or things they don't like, it's easy for us to get wrapped up in the drama too. We get involved. We try to help. We offer our opinions. We take them on, headfirst, until they quite literally become our own problems.

It's not your problem.

You can still care. You can still give love. You can still give advice. You can still feel sad for another. You can still be empathetic without making someone else's problem your own problem.

You don't need to absorb the emotions and energy of someone else. If you do, you will quite literally take on someone else's problem. You will feel all of their emotions like they are your own. Well, they are not yours to have, nor do you want them.

When we have negative thoughts come in, or energy that is draining us, it's easy to try to push it away and not deal. We tell ourselves to stop thinking and get over it. And in some cases, this is all we need when we have those inner-critic type thoughts that we know are completely untrue. (And why the "Schedule Your Thoughts" mantra works so well.)

But in other cases, we really need to sit with that energy because it keeps coming back. It haunts us. It consumes our brains until we do something about it.

If you're feeling some negative energy swirling around you trying to get in, confront it. Ask it where it's coming from. Sit with it. Deal with it. It may not be pretty at first, but it turns into beauty when you're done.

Let the moment of clarity calm you down. And remember, it's not your problem.

Today: Feeling any negative energy? Not sure where it's coming from? Think about others who you may be feeding off of. Are you soaking in their energy instead of giving out yours? Ask yourself if it's really your problem or is it someone else's that you absorbed. The answer may surprise you.

Note: For other coaches, or people who are in the business of helping others with their emotions, this is particularly relevant. You are already intuitive people if you are helping others. So it's easier to absorb energy from clients. Find a way to block other people's negative energy so you don't absorb it.

YOU CAN'T PROTECT
OTHER PEOPLE'S FEELINGS

Why do we feel the need to babysit others?

To protect their feelings.
To keep them out of awkward situations.
To prevent them from hurting.
To make sure they're happy…all the time.

When we do this for others, we neglect ourselves. We make concessions. We ignore our intuitions. We do everything for everyone else except us. And then, we're left with the consequences. *Regret. Shame. Anger. Sadness.*

Basically—we are left with nothing.

This is all because we don't want others to worry, feel uncomfortable, have pain, or have a bad time. We watch over them, like they are babies who can't take care of themselves.

The reality is that they can take care of themselves. We just don't like how they do it. We don't like their behaviors. We don't like their judgments. Or we worry about their behaviors and judgments.

We don't like the idea of the "what if." What could they say? What will they think? What if they have a terrible time and judge me for it? What if they are left in pain? What if they blame me?

So, we try to control it. We try to anticipate any feeling they may have and come up with an answer before they even have it. We try to prevent their feelings. We are way off.

We forget that we can't control others' feelings. Feelings are formed based on your thought filters. Every thought you have goes through a filter of your experiences of life. And every single person in this life has a different filter.

Trying to control others' feelings only causes stress and worry. And the worst—not being yourself.

Be honest with yourself and make decisions based on what you want. At the end of the day, it's about you and your feelings. You can't have feelings for someone else. It's not your problem.

Today: Who are you babysitting? How can you let go of controlling them?

YOU DON'T HAVE TIME FOR THAT

"Do you ever wonder what people say about you behind your back?"

I asked my husband that question. His response couldn't have been more perfect.

"No. I don't have time for that."

I thought about his response and wondered why so many people harp and focus on gossip.

You don't want to be misunderstood. You don't want negative or untrue words affecting your reputation. Basically, you want to be liked. Even more than that though, you want to be loved, adored, and admired. It's unnerving for you to think of others saying bad things behind your back. Ignorance is bliss.

We talked about it again and he said that of course the thoughts enter his mind, but they aren't useful at all to him, so why bother holding on to them? This. Exactly.

Thinking about what other people might be thinking about you is a complete waste of time. Even if you know exactly what they are saying about you behind your back, is thinking about it worth it? Is using your brain power to think about other people's negativity really serving you at all? Is it making you a better person? Or is it just dragging you down to their level?

I know what you're thinking. It's not that easy. Your mind is spinning with anger, especially if you found out someone's been saying false things about you or taken advantage of you. Your mind makes accusations, asks questions, and creates stories until you actually feel it in your body.

Allow yourself to feel. Are you sad, angry, or frustrated? Feel it. Cry or punch a pillow if you need to. Vent to a friend, write in your journal, or do a challenging workout. Make sure you are aware of your feelings and you do something about them.

You need to feel your feelings. Even when they hurt. Even when they sting. Even when they cause you emotional pain. Because if you don't feel them now, they will come back with a vengeance later.*

Not everyone is going to like you. Accept that. But don't let their words or actions affect you. It's not worth it. You're so much better than that.

Today: Is thinking about what someone else is potentially thinking or saying about you serving you in any way? Release your feelings and remind yourself that thinking about other people's opinions is a waste of your precious time.

*Taken from *Unleashed*, my first book. Yes, I quoted myself.

SIDELINE THOSE WHO ARE RUINING YOUR GAME

You know that really amazing feeling that leaves you feeling calm and peaceful with a smile on your face?

- When you meet someone new who totally gets you.
- When you look into your significant other's eyes and see pure love.
- When you have a five-hour phone call with your best friend gossiping and laughing.
- When you finally quit that job that you hate.
- When you indulge in a pedicure and sip on champagne.
- When you run a half marathon after training for so long.
- When you're so engulfed in a book you stay up all night to read it.

Why aren't you having that feeling more often? What has happened to us that we don't do or appreciate the things in life that light us up?

All we do is complain:

I have no time for myself. I'm exhausted. I'm fat. I definitely gained weight. I hate how I look in clothes. I have no social life. I work too much. My husband's driving me crazy. I hate my job. I have no money. I can't afford anything I want.

Oh that list goes on and on and you know it.

Let's start thinking about what we do have. Let's start appreciating it. Let's start bragging about it. Say it aloud. Write it down.

We hide our accomplishments because we don't want to be viewed as conceited or we don't want to get a negative reaction from someone. Essentially, we are hiding ourselves. And how the heck is that making you happy?

If you want to share your happiness with others, then you should be able to. The people who aren't happy for you or don't care what you're doing should have less game time in your life. Put them on the sideline. You don't have to completely kick them out of the game, but maybe they need a time out. Then spend your time with people who get it, who accept you, who are genuinely happy for you, and who don't let their own problems compete with yours. Spend your time with people who will do a touchdown dance with you.

- If you want to run a race, then start talking to people who run races.
- If you want to quit your job and start your own business, then start talking to others who made the leap.
- If you are getting married, then start talking to other bride-to-be's.
- If you want to be a vegan, then start talking to other vegans or people who respect your decision.

Sometimes the only people who get it (and you) are the people going through the same period of life as you. And that's okay. Not everyone will understand. Don't take it personally. Just surround yourself with people who understand. Again, this doesn't mean that you have to cut your family and friends out of your life, but if they aren't supporting your goals or you, then focus less on them and focus more on you and the people who are like you.

You'll be much happier in the end. Then that amazing, warm, smile-filled, comfortable, centered feeling will come more and more.

You deserve it. Why aren't you letting yourself have it?

Today: Sideline people who aren't supportive and find a team you want to join.

DON'T LOWER YOUR STANDARDS

High standards are necessary. High expectations (of others) are a waste of time. Standards empower you to take ownership of what's happening in your life whereas expectations give responsibility to something else.

Standards are your code for living. These are your morals, merits, and principles. You have complete control of your standards. They are comprised of who you are, what's important to you and what's not, what your boundaries are, and what's tolerable. Have high standards. Embody them. Own them.

Expectations are what you want other people to do. They exist outside of you and are filled with shoulds. Expectations are completely based on others.

No wonder you don't like it when someone doesn't live up to your expectations. You want them to act the way you want them to act or the way you would act. Remember that no one acts the same way, as everyone has different world views and experiences that create their personalities.

The problem arises when people tell you to lower your expectations, and you lower your standards instead.

When you set expectations, you are predicting the future behaviors of other people. How can you predict the future?

When you set standards, you are ensuring that you give and receive what you deserve. You are creating boundaries that dictate who is in your life and what you accept from yourself and others.

If someone isn't living up to your standards, why are you keeping this person in your life? Why are you tolerating certain actions? Why are you going against your beliefs because of someone else? Why are you keeping friends who drag you down? Why are you continuing a disrespectful relationship?

You deserve to have a great quality of life, amazing friends, true love, companionship, and respect.

Not everyone is the same as you. You can't change that. You have to accept others as they are, but that doesn't mean you have to think or act like they do either. That doesn't mean you have to put up with things you don't like. That doesn't mean you have to lower to their level.

You have choices. Choices in where you live, how you act, who you surround yourself with, who you date, how you value yourself, and who you are. You have the choice every single day.

Remember that you are who you are and you shouldn't have to lower any of your standards to feel better. Detach yourself from anyone who isn't bringing value to your life.

Today: Have you defined your standards? Make a list now. What are your beliefs, principles, and morals in life? Once you've defined them, is anyone in your life not living up to your standards? Are they worth keeping in your life?

Note: Having high expectations for yourself is necessary if you want to achieve your goals. But if you set expectations for yourself, then you are responsible for creating the path to meet or exceed those expectations. This is different from having high expectations for others who you cannot control. You can control yourself.

DISAPPOINTMENT DOESN'T HAVE TO EXIST

You have high standards. You have lofty goals. You have premier visions. You expect a great deal from yourself. And there's nothing wrong with any of that. You're respecting yourself. You're striving to be better. But sometimes you can't help but feel disappointed. You let yourself down. You created an idea of perfection and you didn't live up to that idea. Know this though…

Disappointment is imaginary.

If you focus on the learning process that comes with the journey, then you can prevent disappointment. It's not going to be perfect along the way. Motivational speaker Brendon Burchard says that you are always perfecting, not being perfect.

Some people may say that your expectations for yourself are too high, but lowering your expectations doesn't solve disappointment. Why would you lower your expectations for yourself when you want to achieve great things? Why would you lower your expectations for yourself when you want to turn your vision into your reality?

You will always be learning and evolving. That's how you get better. You may struggle and be challenged, but feeling bad about yourself doesn't serve you at all. Be satisfied with what you are doing and who you are. If you are always doing your best, you won't be disappointed.

This also applies to other people. If you feel disappointed by someone else, remember that not everyone thinks or acts the same way as you.

So, stop taking it personally. The situation you have with another has nothing to do with you and everything to do with that person. Reflect on the personality and behavior of this person to understand and live according to their world view. Again, not everyone acts as you do. People express attention, care, and appreciation differently.

As soon as you can embrace this concept, it's easier to release disappointment.

Does thinking about others' actions serve you? Decide not to let disappointment win. Allow yourself to feel good about you and disappointment won't exist in your life.

Today: Have you felt disappointed? How can you change your idea of disappointment so that it can be prevented?

RELATIONSHIPS ARE NOT HARD

"Relationships are hard." This is what people would tell me constantly when I was going through a rough time in a relationship.

"Relationships are **not** hard." This is what people told me after a break-up because "we shouldn't have had to work that hard."

Needless to say, I was very conflicted on the advice I was receiving. After analyzing and piecing together advice that actually applied to me, I realized why people told me relationships are hard.

Relationships require work, but a sign of a good relationship is when the work you are applying results in a better relationship. The relationship becomes hard when you continue to work on the same issue and see no progress.

Relationships are only hard if you make them hard. If you see no growth or advancement. If you question yourself. If you are not acting like yourself. If you lose yourself. If you fear the potential outcomes. If you feel anxious about the future. If you think your partner will change. If you try to change your partner.

Relationships are designed to help you grow and evolve, individually. Relationships are assignments. They act as a mirror into your own life, bringing awareness to behaviors and characteristics that you may have never noticed before.

You also have to accept who the other person is. You cannot be in a relationship and expect your partner to change. People only change if they are willing to. Why would you enter into a relationship with someone you want to change?

Relationships are meant to be easy. If you find yourself saying that relationships are hard, look deeper.

They are supposed to be fulfilling, supportive, loving, and happy. Yes, there are arguments, rough patches, and issues. But they shouldn't consume your entire being. They shouldn't break you or your couple easily.

You have a choice in every relationship. A choice to make it work. A choice to stay. A choice to leave. A choice to change. A choice to never change. A choice to communicate.

If you're having the same argument repeatedly or if previous issues resurface constantly, you're not working on anything. You're glossing over the subject. Someone's not willing to work on that issue. If there isn't any progress, it won't get any better.

The kind of relationship you have affects the rest of your life. As soon as you find clarity in who you are and what you want in a relationship, you will feel liberated. You will feel confident in expressing your needs and wants and won't settle for anything less.

Leaving a relationship that is not working is not a failure. It's being strong enough and brave enough to face the truth. It's about understanding who you are. It's about knowing how you want to live. It's about acting on what is true to your heart.

Most of the time, you know the answer, but you try to look for evidence against it to prevent yourself and the other person from hurting. Staying together can feel so much easier than letting go. That's common. Separating will hurt. But a small amount of hurt in exchange for a lifetime of happiness is totally worth it.

Today: How do you feel about your relationship with your partner? Is it hard or easy? Do you make progress on disagreements?

ATTRACT YOUR IDEAL RELATIONSHIP

I'll never find anyone else.
No one will understand me the same way.
It's annoying to repeat my whole life story all over again to someone new.
No one else will find me funny or beautiful.
I'm never going to love again.

If your best friend was saying these statements to you after a break-up, divorce, or a long period of being single, how would you react?

You'd probably say something like this…

You will find someone else who is better for you.
Someone else will understand you, even deeper.
It's fun to talk about your life experiences again to someone new.
Many others will love your amazing qualities.
You will fall madly in love, perhaps even a love you didn't know before.

So why are you telling yourself all of those statements above? Why are you talking to yourself like that if you wouldn't allow your best friend to say those things?

Believe in the possibilities. What if…everything works out better than you ever imagined?

Have faith. If you don't have faith in yourself, then nothing you want will happen. Your mindset can produce miracles. Miracles are shifts in perception. How can you shift your mindset right now to produce what you want? Are you clear on what you want?

Clarity and focus are two of the main qualities of people who achieve their desires. Dreaming alone doesn't turn frogs into princes. You need to have a vision so when what you want arrives in front of your face, you see a prince, not a frog.

Here is my favorite exercise for finding clarity in your future partner and relationship.

Today: Make THE IDEAL PARTNER LIST. The list is a compilation of all the characteristics you want in your next relationship and partner. Using the categories I listed below, write in what you ideally want and how you want to feel. Make it specific. I cannot stress enough how much you have to be ultra specific. I made this list after a breakup and my now husband walked off the page and into my life. Exactly every single thing about him and our relationship is on my list (except for one minor thing that we joke about now—ask me about it).

Use these categories (and feel free to add in more):

Physical characteristics (e.g., 6'2", blue eyes, athletic build…)

Personality and Mentality (e.g., outgoing, calm, isn't scared of being vulnerable, affectionate…)

Career and Ambition (e.g., established in career, values work/life balance…)

Family/Friends Life (e.g., knows he wants children, has good friends, respectful of family...)

Adventure and Travel (e.g., loves to travel, open to moving, likes to explore...)

Don't Want... (Write all the things you don't want and then turn each don't into a positive statement. Example: I don't want him to be closed off. He is open and honest with me and we will be open and honest together.)

Our Lifestyle Together (e.g., Always happy to see one another. Work hard, play hard. Active adventure days and lazy at home days.)

Our Relationship Together (e.g., We express our feelings. We listen. We laugh, we cry. We love.)

Desires to Create and Experience Together (e.g., Create a life of happiness. Experience the comfort of home with one another.)

After you've made this list, tuck it away somewhere safe. Try not to only see frogs hopping around you, but look deeper to find that charming partner who could very well be in your life right now but you just didn't notice it.

Now, you have the gift of clarity.

FIND FREEDOM

CONTROL. CHALLENGE. CHANGE. BELIEVE.
OPPORTUNITY. FOCUS.

You're scared. Of the future. Of the unknown. Of the challenge. Of the outcome.

You feel like you don't have control. You continue to worry. You make up scenarios. You feel stuck.

You want this to end. You want to feel normal again. You want to use your energy on the things that matter. It's just so hard to make your mind stop spinning.

If you actually started living now, in this moment, and only focused on today, imagine your potential. Imagine what you would actually get done. Imagine what your tomorrow could look like.

What if you stopped caring so much?
What if you saw the opportunities instead of the failures?
What if you had more control than you thought?
What if change actually turned out good?
What if you stopped shoulding?
What if you focused on the outcome and not how you were going to get there?
What if you lived in the now instead of in the future?
What if you challenged your fears?
What if you tried?

Worrying about the future only wastes your time. Why? Because it hasn't happened yet and you can't predict it no matter how hard you try. Worrying only leads to believing in the worst case scenarios. And when you believe enough in something, it comes true.

It's time to start believing in the possibilities. Start believing in today. Today is all you have. Yesterday doesn't matter. Tomorrow doesn't matter. Live today, hour by hour. Don't let fear stop you. Use it to propel you.

Freedom, then, will be yours. Use the next eight mantras to liberate yourself.

STOP CARING SO MUCH
RELEASE THE PATTERN
YOU CAN CONTROL THE OUTCOME
CHANGE IS GOOD
STOP SHOULDING
FIND COMFORT IN GETTING LOST
CENTER YOURSELF
CONQUER YOUR FEAR

STOP CARING SO MUCH

Stop putting extra weight on things that don't need the extra pounds. (Including you. Pun intended.) When you think too much, your mind spins stories. Believing those stories can cause you to ignore opportunities, live in fear, and miss life.

These "what ifs" are detrimental to your well-being. What might happen. What might be said. What might the outcome be.

The "what ifs" create future tripping. Future tripping is when you let your mind spin out of control with every scenario that could potentially happen to you. Only none of these situations has happened to you yet. The scenarios are completely made up. Yup, they're false. Have they happened yet? Nope. So they're not true. They are big fat lies. Why are you lying to yourself?

The truth is that you never know what could happen. Going on a date with someone doesn't mean you'll get married. Launching your services doesn't mean you'll be scrutinized. Trying a new workout doesn't mean you'll hate it and never see results. Quitting your job doesn't mean you're a failure.

Instead of looking at all the negative things that could happen, look at some of the opportunities that could arise. Maybe that date will have a friend who is perfect for you (or maybe he's perfect for you). Maybe you'll have a waitlist for your new service. Maybe you'll love your new workout and be inspired to exercise. Maybe your new job is a dream come true.

If you continue to say it won't happen, then it won't. That's sad because it can happen. So next time you start future tripping, catch yourself. Ask yourself if anything you just told yourself is true. Is it true or is it based on a cleverly-spun mind story?

In the age of "let it go" and "keep calm and carry on/meditate/down tequila" we are inundated with phrases to help us deal with it and move on. What are all these phrases really telling us though? Stop caring so darn much.

Of course you care, you're human! But when you care to the point of constant nerves and brain spins that keep you up at night, then it's time to re-evaluate what you're focusing on.

Imagine sitting on a couch and a person is next to you who is completely made up of your thoughts. When something is bothering you, listen to that person talk for an hour without responding. If this were an actual person, you would likely have to walk away after ten minutes because you wouldn't be able to listen to the constant spewing of made up stories. Now remember that it is you and your stories. The same way that you walked away from the person on the couch, walk away from those thoughts.

Whatever you obsess about creates energy. You become that energy. You send out that energy. So you will only attract what you're obsessing about (e.g., no money) and other people who have that same energy. Why the heck would you want to attract bad energy?

Your life doesn't have to stay on repeat. You have all the power to have the life you want and get what you want. That power starts in your mind.

Today: Catch yourself when you're future tripping. Is it true? Has it happened? Or is it a big maybe? Imagine your thoughts as a person sitting next to you. What would your advice be for that person?

RELEASE THE PATTERN

Your life doesn't have to stay on repeat. Just because it happened that way before doesn't mean it will happen that way again. You can change outcomes, actions, and circumstances by the way you think.

I was gazing out at the Atlantic Ocean in Biarritz, France after a humbling surf session. My husband and I had flown to this beautiful southwest town in France early in the morning and wasted no time on our first day of vacation. At 10pm, I was shivering as I peeled off my wet suit and waited for my husband and brother-in-law to come out of the ocean.

Surfing is a new sport for me, which definitely subscribes to the "practice makes perfect" mentality. I had surfed for the first time in Bali, but had many days to practice. When I arrived in Biarritz, I had memories of pure joy as I stood on the board riding waves. As I laid on the board paddling my arms off to catch a wave in Biarritz, I realized that the art of surfing was not going to come back to me immediately. Damn that "it's like riding a bike, you never forget" analogy.

Cold, tired, and feeling very uncool, I sat on the beach thinking about how many people believe that if something happens a certain way, it will always happen that way. That it will never change because it has "always happened that way."

This spans so many different topics in our lives:

I'm going to get sick on the plane because I did last time.
I'll never lose weight because the latest diet trend didn't work.
I'll never trust a man again because one cheated on me.
I froze while negotiating with a new client so I'm not taking anymore calls.
I fell off my surf board every time I stood up, I'll never be good.

Just because it happened one way before does not mean it will happen that way again. There is a reason for the good old falling off a horse analogy. (Finally, a good one!) You have to get back up. Whether you had an embarrassing moment, crazy client, motion sickness, or a boyfriend who treated you like garbage—none of this means that it will all repeat itself.

The only way it will repeat itself is if you let it. If you're afraid to open up in a new relationship because you got burned in the past, then you're not going to get very far in the new one. If you don't think you can ever enjoy exercising or be able to fit it in your schedule because it didn't work before, then you won't.

Those thoughts are holding you back. That's all they are—thoughts that aren't you. As it turns out, you can do whatever you think you can do. *And you can't do what you think you can't.* Your life doesn't have to stay on repeat.

Today: What pattern do you allow to repeat in your life? Does it always have to happen that way? Or are you letting it?

YOU CAN CONTROL THE OUTCOME

You're questioning…
Thinking…
What if'ing…
Doubting…

Thoughts plague your mind so intensely that your body feels like it is going to shut down. You feel frozen, just like Elsa* but without the fancy ice castle.

Thinking you don't have control is an illusion. You have so much more control than you think. The moment you stop thinking, doubting, and worrying about something, it happens for you.

You stop thinking about finding a new job. One comes to you.
You stop thinking about finding the right man. One comes to you.
You stop thinking about the best website name. One comes to you.

Not like magic. Though wouldn't that be nice? Law of Attraction worshippers may disagree. Though it may feel like magic, it isn't magic.

When we stop worrying, we stop sending out that nervous energy. The "what ifs." The "overwhelm." The "it'll never happen for me." The "I don't deserve it."

When you think that way, of course nothing you want will come to you. You are actually declaring that it won't happen for you and that you don't deserve it. Subconsciously, you are pushing away everything you want by taking the wrong actions or worse, inaction. So why would it come to you if you've been pushing it away? Why would it happen to you if you haven't been taking the opportunities coming to you?

You're believing these doubts and worries. What you believe turns into reality and reality is based on the actions you take. If you're believing negative thoughts, you're acting on them. Then that becomes your reality.

Your thoughts are manageable and controllable. The unfortunate thing about the self-sabotaging thoughts is that we can turn any event into a nightmare pretty quickly if it overwhelms us.

Thinking you don't have control is an illusion. You have so much more control than you think. You actually have control of what you think.

Today: What's your big worry? Break it down into small pieces. Tackle each piece at a time. It will be much less overwhelming.

*Elsa is the character in the animation movie *Frozen* that has special powers to freeze everything. It's extremely popular with the under seven crowd for anyone who has found this book in 2115. Though adults are secretly obsessed as well.

CHANGE IS GOOD

Change can be the best thing to happen to you. But that's not what you want to hear, because change means change. It means your routine has been tampered with. It means something different, something uncomfortable, or something that you may not like at all. It's diving headfirst into the scary world of the unknown.

But what if you never try anything that requires change?

What if you never...

...move to a new city because it's too much work?
...learn a new language because it's too hard?
...flirt with the bartender who winked at you because you feel silly?
...let yourself fall in love because you're scared to get hurt?
...speak up when you know someone is wrong because you are afraid of what she'll say?
...write an article for the magazine because you feel like a fraud?
...teach a dance class because you feel like you're not good enough?
...be yourself because you think no one will like the real you?

What if you never try any of that? What if you keep living in the status-quo, same old, nothing new life that you don't want anymore?

What if change brought you new opportunities? And not only new, but better. It's often not the actual change that you have such a hard time with, it's wrapping your mind around the change.

So what if you actually do it? Ask for help. Put your name out there. Change your scenery. Fall in love.

Would it be worth it?

Today: What do you wish you would try or change right now, but you're too scared? Try it. At least let yourself think about what your life would be like if it worked.

STOP SHOULDING

We can make things way more complicated than they need to be. We can take something that can be simple and easy and turn it into the plague.

This happens at work, at home, in relationships, and often when you are wrapped up in only one solution, one idea, one process, or one way of being.

We should a lot. That's the problem. We should when it comes to the kind of job we are expected to take. We should when it comes to doing favors for others. We should when it comes to choosing a life partner. We should when it comes to planning a wedding. And we should a lot especially when it comes to exercise.

We should run. We should do yoga. We should lift weights. We should kickbox the fat right out of us six days a week.

Maybe you do those shoulds for a few days, or maybe even a few weeks. Then what happens? Those shoulds fly right out the window. Why? Because you never wanted to do them in the first place. They were shoulds. Not wants. Not needs.

Let's take exercise as an example. You know the health benefits—mind and body—that exercise brings to you. You know that it makes you lose weight, tone up, and look sexy. You know you'll feel better, sleep better, and prevent disease. But you think it has to be done a certain way. That you must kick your own ass repeatedly get any results.

Sure, certain things require certain efforts. If you want to run a race, do a triathlon, or complete an electric shock mud race–you must train hard. If you want to seriously lose weight, you need to watch what you're eating and drinking.

You want to exercise. You need to exercise. But you think you should exercise a certain way. If you want to lose ten pounds, release some stress, feel sexy in your own skin, and have a happier outlook on life (basically create a lifestyle change)—then you need to exercise in a way that you want to. Think about a form of exercise that doesn't feel like the "should" exercise you've been thinking about. What's a way to exercise that allows you to freely move your body and let those endorphins flow without even realizing it? Eliminating the should is how you create change.

Why are you shoulding? Is it the societal pressure? Are you trying to respect your culture? Is it based on your family's experiences and way of thinking? Is it based on what your friends and colleagues are doing? Are you shoulding because of other people? Why are you so concerned with what others are doing and thinking?

Focus on yourself. Turn your shoulds into wants.

Today: Right now, I urge you to do a workout that feels good, that you want to do, and that you actually look forward to doing—instead of pushing it off until the next day, and the next, and the next. It can be anything. A workout doesn't mean you have to get super intense and crazy. Start with some stretches. Start with a walk. Start with a dance session in your living room. Just start.

FIND COMFORT IN GETTING LOST

I get lost. Beaucoup. I prefer the grid system of New York City, my cherished home of over six years, to the winding streets of Paris because it's easier to find my way. I like to be efficient.

Getting lost in the maze of streets in Paris has had its pros and cons though. Yes, it's how I've found cute alleyways, the organic store, and a wine cave dedicated to champagne. It's also how I've been thirty minutes late to lunch meetings, tried to get into the wrong apartment buildings, and exhausted myself in the summer heat (that isn't supposed to happen in Paris) by walking a mile in the wrong direction. But instead of focusing on the negatives, I choose to let it be a shift in my mindset to be open to other possibilities.

Because I get lost, I find so much. I wouldn't have discovered anything new if I had been controlling my direction the entire time. This is life. You have paths and plans set, but does precisely following that path stone by stone get you to the outcome you want?

Become more comfortable with getting lost. Not knowing your way. Discovering little corners. Sneaking off to enjoy the afternoon outside. Embracing the unknown. Listening to the ideas of others. Allowing the path to illuminate for you.

You can get so focused on the "how" (how anything will happen) that you panic if you lose control of the path that (you think) takes you there. You avoid. You procrastinate. You quit. You stress. You wake up with a pit in your stomach every morning.

Allowing things to flow, weave, stop, start, and saunter can give you a greater outcome than you ever could have imagined. Sometimes you have to let it unfold naturally instead of controlling every moment. But you have to be okay with letting it go naturally first.

It's not easy, and sometimes it has to happen by accident. But it will be the best accident that you could have.

Today: How are you going to let go of the "how" this week? What can you lose in order to find what you need?

CENTER YOURSELF

Anticipation of the unknown can make the most confident person crumble. Especially if living in the present moment is a foreign concept.

We all have nerves, but some of us can experience them so much more severely than others. Sometimes to the point of physical pain—headaches so severe you can't see, muscles so tight in your back you can't move, or stomach aches so painful you can't eat.

These nerves are a build-up of past emotions and feelings. They keep piling on top of one another until your body gives out or you just give up. (Also commonly known as burnout.) What's causing them? Anticipation.

If you're always worrying about the future, you will live your entire life in fear—an entire life not lived in the present but in a future that doesn't exist and may never exist.

Anticipation is wonderful combination of waiting, assumptions, and fear. The unknown is in front of you and you have no freaking clue what's going to happen. All you know is that this in-between time is hurting you. You just want it to be over. You want to be there already. You don't want to think about it anymore.

Maybe you're waiting for your presentation to be over on how you're reorganizing the entire company, your boss to leave the office so you're not asked to do one more thing at 9pm, your sick loved one to bounce back to life, your application to be accepted, the emails in your inbox to flood in after you launch a program, the plane to take off...

Whatever it is, you're waiting with no answers. You can't rush the time, even though you desperately want to. You want to know your fate. You want it to be over, or to never end.

The fear that comes with anticipation and the unknown can cripple us. It can keep you right where you are—never able to move forward. It can make you doubt everything. It can make you stop living, stop being you, and stop chasing the life you want and deserve. It can make you ungrateful for what's going on in your life right now. It can make you give up. It can make you never truly live in this moment—never enjoy and appreciate what's around you at this time, right now.

We've all been told to "Live in the present moment!" and "Be here, now!" and "Stop worrying!" But most of the time, that it is easier said than done. You know that you should focus on right now. You know that focusing on this moment makes you happy, centered, and less stressed.

How do you do this though? How do you start living in the present?

Focus on one hour at a time. When I find myself future-tripping like crazy, I tell myself to stop and just think about the next hour. What am I doing in the next hour?

I only think about that hour. When that hour is up, I move on to the next hour. This has saved me so much time that I used to spend thinking about the future.

Be grateful for this moment you have right now to read this book, to have a glass of champagne with your best friends, to work on an exciting project, to eat a healthy breakfast. Focus on it and enjoy it. Be grateful for it.

If you're always worrying about the future, you will live your entire life in fear. What kind of life is that? Not one that I want.

Today: Part 1: What's holding you back? What is holding you in anticipation? Just identify it. Part 2: Try living one hour at a time.

CONQUER YOUR FEAR

You have control.

Those three words echo throughout my brain whenever I ski down a big mountain.

If you've read any of my Monday Mantra emails about my skiing adventures or just heard me talk about them, they're pretty funny (now). They usually include me tumbling down a mountain, falling into snow banks, and tears. Sad tears.

I only learned how to ski in my late 20s, which brings out all kinds of fears versus the people who learned how to ski at age two (ahem…my husband). While my husband has been the best teacher I've ever had, his teaching methods go like this: Get Diana to the very top of an extremely high mountain and tell her to go down. In all fairness, the first time we skied together he thought I had skied way more than I did, though I did tell him I had next-to-zero experience. That's besides the point. Back to the mountain. I went to the top and started to go down. This resulted in getting buried in snow banks and sad tears. As soon as he saw that, he realized he needed to give me a proper lesson. Once he did and I grasped the technique, the game changed.

Back to my mantra. The next time we went skiing, we were with a bunch of friends who are expert skiers. On the second day, I was the only woman who went with all the guys. On the second chair lift up the mountain after doing a green circle, they said to me, "With how well you're skiing today, you can totally do the Showcase trail down the mountain today."

Me: "Is that a blue square?"
Guys: "Yes, you can definitely do it."
Me: "I don't know."

For the skiing novices out there: In the USA, green circles are easy, blue squares are more difficult, and black diamonds are for the crazy people who think it's fun to go down steep, icy mountains. Me...one day.

I was scared.

As the gondola took us higher and higher, I gazed at the view of beautiful snow-covered trees, thinking about how I was very happy with myself that I just mastered a green circle trail. I questioned attempting the blue square trail that was specifically called "Showcase" because it is under the gondola so people can watch you. And that's when I told myself to stop thinking and just do it.

You know my philosophy by now: When you think too much, you can cause your mind to spiral out of control and make up stories that are completely false.

"You have control." Those three words took me down a much more difficult trail with steeper hills and little bumps, without falling.

I felt good. Ready. Fearless. We went up again to do the same trail. I totally dominated it. I went at speeds that normally sent me into a panic and cruised down the hills effortlessly.

I got to the bottom, stopped, and realized that I had just conquered a huge fear. I actually enjoyed myself.

Remember that you always have control of your mind—and you will make it to the end.

Today: Think about a time that you were faced with a challenge and decided to just go for it and conquer your fear. How can you use that experience to conquer a fear you're battling now?

FEEL INVINCIBLE

STRENGTH. TENACITY. BALANCE. POSSIBILITY. PRODUCTIVITY. PRIORITY.

You have bold goals, lofty dreams, and piercing visions. You know you can make a difference. You want to be legendary.

You want it so bad it's all you can think about.

Something's holding you back though. You're not acting on your priorities. You're not putting yourself first. You're not believing in yourself fully. You're not starting.

What are you waiting for?

What you do today is who you are next week. Start making decisions. Start giving yourself more credit. Start believing that you are stronger than you think. Start.

Your legacy is created every single day. Don't push it off. Don't worry about other people. Don't worry about timelines. Don't focus on the past. Don't fall down from failure. Don't worry about things that haven't happened yet.

You can have it all. You just have to know what *it all* means to you. You have to start.

Use the next twelve mantras to stop wanting and start acting. Feel invincible.

YOU CAN HAVE IT ALL
GIVE YOURSELF MORE CREDIT
YOU ARE STRONGER THAN YOU THINK YOU ARE
START NOW
FAILURE DOESN'T HAVE TO EXIST
PUSH PAST THE FEAR
CREATE YOUR LEGACY
SCHEDULE YOUR THOUGHTS
FOCUS ON YOUR PRIORITIES
DOING NOTHING CAN BE PRODUCTIVE
STOP DOUBTING YOURSELF
YOU ARE INCOMPARABLE

SANITY IS SEXY

YOU CAN HAVE IT ALL

You can do it all and you can have it all. First though, I have a few questions for you to answer:

- What is "it all" anyway?
- Why would anyone tell you that you couldn't do it or have it?
- Why are you telling yourself you can't do it or have it?

Having it all does not mean you equally divide all aspects of your life into the same percentages. It is not about distributing time evenly for everything you want to do. It is about defining it for yourself, asking yourself what you want, and figuring out how to incorporate it into your day. If you can do two minutes per day of something for yourself, only yourself, then you have what you want. You are putting yourself first for those two minutes. You're doing something for you.

When at a women's networking event, I noticed a skeptical look from a mother of a two-year-old who is working full time and barely does anything for herself.

As we continued talking, I watched her slowly realize that she did have some semblance of balance. I said to her, "You came out tonight, didn't you?" She said yes, and that she had decided to bike to the event on her own as her "me time." She felt so good biking around Paris by herself to go to an event where all she had to think about was herself.

That's balance. Taking just a little bit of time—whatever time you have. Some days it's two minutes. Some days it's two hours. It's taking that time and using it to feel better.

Many companies and experts are trying to define work/life balance now. Some say it doesn't exist at all. Can others really create balance for you though? Only you can create it for yourself. Only you know your life and what's a priority for you.

You can have it all, providing that you know what "it all" means in your life. Define it.

Today: Define what "having it all" means in your life. Make a list of things you want to do and brainstorm how to incorporate them little by little in your life.

GIVE YOURSELF MORE CREDIT

You aren't giving yourself enough credit...

As a business owner
As a wife or a husband
As a mother or a father
As a child
As a friend
As an employee
As an expert

You play down your strengths. You don't pat yourself on the back for a job well done. You don't fully receive compliments. You say it was "no big deal." You go along, day by day, doing what you do, without giving it a second thought. And when you do give it a second thought, it's not always a good thought. You wonder how you could have done it better and you let your mind spin stories, convincing yourself you aren't good enough. Convincing yourself that you have no idea what you're doing.

But actually, you do know what you are doing.

You are damn good at your job—as a spouse, friend, parent, business owner—as you. You just don't always celebrate it.

You're not perfect. Your confidence levels waver. Your mind plays tricks on you. But remember that you do know what you're doing. You're making a difference.

Life has ups and downs and it's completely normal to fluctuate emotions. One bad day with your spouse or kids, one bad review of your book, or one bad interview at the job you really wanted can bring you down and make you stop believing in yourself. You feel down, lacking motivation to continue. You wonder when it's going to change, when you're going to get better, or when it's going to be your turn to thrive.

If you feel down or if you feel like you need a boost of motivation, remember what you've done. Remember how you've mastered your job, your life, and your business. Remember all of the challenging experiences you've been through that you overcame.

Remember what you continue to do every day. It has become so normal for you that you don't see it as special anymore. You have the gift, remember that.

Today: Write down what you've done in life that makes you feel really accomplished.

(Helped your spouse through a difficult time at work. Taught your child how to count to ten in another language. Gave dozens of clients hope. Made an impression on the CEO. Finished your degree with perfect grades.)

If you're not getting anywhere with that, ask someone else who you can trust and who has been following your journey. Others admire you; ask them to help you.

YOU ARE STRONGER THAN
YOU THINK YOU ARE

I'm not motivated when I'm bad at something. I'm motivated when I start to master something.

I exclaimed this statement when I started learning the French language, but I quickly realized that this applies to most of us when it comes to exercise (and pretty much any other thing you are trying to learn).

I'm motivated to do more push-ups when I can squeeze out two more than last time. I'm motivated to run faster when I feel invincible after my last run. I'm motivated to try a new crazy abdominal exercise when I see the results in the mirror.

When you are exercising, your mind plays tricks on you. It says you can't do it. It says you aren't strong enough. It asks you who you think you are trying to twist your spine and abs into a reverse crunch.

You are stronger than you think you are. Your body shows you something else though. It actually shows you that you can do it. And when your body absolutely cannot do it, it surely lets you know. You reward your body with rest and fuel, because you know you reached its capacity.

This is why it is so hard for some people to start exercise plans. Your mind thinks you can't do it. Your mind tells you that you will be really bad at it—that you'll never be able to run a mile, that you won't keep up with the rest of the class, that you'll embarrass yourself trying to attempt a push-up.

The truth is that you can do it, but you have to start it in order to believe it. If you don't start, then you can't show your mind that you can do it. The trick is to start slowly with small goals. Hit those small goals, get better, and stay motivated.

Today: What is your mind telling you that you can't do right now? Why is it wrong?

START NOW

You won't complete anything if you don't start now. Complaining, venting, and wishing do nothing for you. What helps? Starting. Acting. Making a decision.

The main source of our stress and anxiousness is indecision. Start making some decisions.

All of those outstanding things that keep building up are holding you back. If you don't make any decisions, then they will continue to be there, haunting you until you completely lose your mind or actually start doing something about it.

Want to start an exercise routine? Start moving your body. Now. Move it, shake it, run it, bike it, dance it. Move.

Want to start eating healthier? Choose a healthy recipe (look on my Pinterest board), buy the ingredients, and make that healthy meal tonight.

Want to go on a big trip? Pick out a sexy place you want to visit, research how much it costs, and start saving. If you have the money (or don't but don't care), book the plane ticket.

Want to do something different this weekend or visit friends? Make a phone call, pick a date, and stick to it.

No more: "what ifs" "maybes" "laters" "can'ts" or "shoulds."

If you want something, really seriously want it, then start doing it.

It doesn't have to be big or perfect. That's what stops us. We want everything to be perfect—the perfect weather to run outside, the new top from the latest fancy yoga brand, the new season (when summer comes…), the new year (January 1…), the dreamy Instagram-able vacation plan…

We wait for everything to line up perfectly. But guess what? Nothing's going to line up if you don't act.

I was scared out of my mind to run a half marathon in 2013. Every possible demeaning thought literally ran through my brain. But I started it and I finished it because I wanted to prove to myself that I could run 13.1 miles.

Was I scared to start the training? Yes.
Did I start the training? Yes.
Did I give up during training even though I had bad days? No.
Did I let my thoughts make me so anxious that I barely made it to the start line? Hell no! (Well, there were a lot of nerves, but I never thought of quitting.)

Want to run a race, swim a mile, or start a new sport? Then start running, start swimming, and start playing that sport.

Want to start your own business? Set aside one hour per day to brainstorm about that business and start writing a plan. Hire a coach to help you.

You don't have to be perfect. You don't have to be the most amazing runner to start running. You don't have to be an Olympic swimmer to start swimming. You don't need to know everything about starting a blog to start one.

Too many times we let these thoughts of comparison, perfection, and fear get in the way of doing what we actually want to do.

What's stopping you? What's holding you back from doing what you want? What are you waiting for?

Put yourself first. Don't wait on anyone else or anything else.

Be honest with yourself. Then start. You may fall, you may hurt, and you may not get it right the first time.

Starting and trying something that you want to do outweighs not doing it at all. Make it happen.

Today: What are you going to start right now that you've been dreaming about but not doing?

FAILURE DOESN'T HAVE TO EXIST

Failure doesn't have to exist. You have the power to turn a failure into success.

I often talk to women who have beautiful souls. Women who want to change people's lives. Women who want to help. Women who have overcome obstacles. Women who are expanding every day.

These women also happen to be in waist-deep, muddy pools of fear. They are scared. Scared their businesses won't be successful. Scared they won't be able to show their kids the world. Scared that they'll be judged. Scared they'll be ignored. Scared they'll fail.

What is failure though? Can you answer that question?

Failure only exists in your mind. Only you have the power to fail. You define failure. You can make shifts and changes when your life isn't going the way you want in order to put it back on the right path.

If no one buys your product, you can make a small change to make it more appealing. You can ask for feedback and find out what will make people purchase it. You can shift it ever so slightly to turn it into something that works.

Have tenacity. Learn from perceived failures, but don't focus on them. That's trying to change the past. You can't change the past, but you can learn for the future. When you have a failure, write out everything that went wrong in your eyes. Then, next to each statement, write how you can do it better next time.

You don't fail. You learn. You shift. You pivot. You change the course. You keep moving. You try again.

If you give up, then success was never yours to begin with.

Today: Where can you make a shift to create a better life, a better business, or a better relationship? Where can you turn a perceived failure into a success?

PUSH PAST THE FEAR

With big ambitions comes fear. Pushing past the fear brings bigger ambitions.

That was a text I sent a friend. I even text in mantras now.

Your confidence level can be based on how often you push past self-doubt.

How do you push past self-doubt?

Try this conversation with yourself. Here's what usually happens in my brain for dramatic effect.

Question 1: Why are you doubting yourself?
Answer 1: _____
(Me: Hmm, I'm scared.)

Question 2: Why are you scared?
Answer 2: _____
(Me: I'm scared of feeling invisible, not good enough, sounding like an idiot—ya know, the usual fears that run through my brain.)

Question 3: Are you serious? Get over it. You know you are fantastic. The only way to get over this is by doing it. What if you don't do it? Then you'll regret it and feel even worse. Why are you letting fear dictate your life?
Answer 3: _____
(Me: Yes, you have a point. Ya know what, you're right! Okay I'm totally going to rock this! Hell yea!)

Sometimes you just need a big swift kick in the ass to get yourself going again instead of wallowing in self-doubt, fear, and those addictive chocolate-dipped-oreos.

See, your fears don't always make much sense when you say them aloud to yourself or to someone else. They're usually unworthy of your time and energy.

The fear may keep coming up over and over again. That's okay. That means it's there for a reason and you may have to dig a bit deeper to find out why it has become a trigger for you. Sometimes all you need is the awareness of the fear to overcome it and move on to the next step. Believe in yourself. Welcome the possibilities.

Today: Follow questions 1-3 and kick doubt to the curb.

CREATE YOUR LEGACY

You can't live your legacy. You create your legacy through action.

The priest said this as he spoke at a funeral. Only this wasn't just any funeral. This was a funeral for a woman who has touched thousands of people and inspired tens of thousands of people, if not more.

This woman's legacy is known by most of the Greek community in the United States of America. She taught Greek folk dancing as the founder of the Hellenic Dancers of New Jersey, a group of young adult Greek Americans who perpetuate their heritage through performing regional folk dances of Greece. This group has performed for presidents and royalty, received awards, and sent dancers to the 2004 Opening Ceremony at the Olympics in Greece.

We were her students, in life and in dance. As my mother eloquently stated, "An era has ended with Mrs. C's passing. She was a unique woman—brilliant, talented, vibrant, and giving. A teacher of more than dance. She taught pride in our heritage. She taught discipline, responsibility, and commitment. She taught the meaning of love and friendship. She will be missed but not forgotten."

She not only taught ages 9 through 50 the Greek folk dances and hand-sewed every single one of our traditional costumes (which she researched and perfected to replicate every region of Greece), she instilled in us our culture. She taught us discipline and commitment from a young age. She knew how to give us the perfect scolding look with love. She was more proud of us every single performance. She got every girl to wear the reddest of red lipstick without a fuss during every performance. She provided the platform for us to create lifetime bonds and friendships, and in some cases, marriages.

She always gave. She always did. She always acted with passion.

I wouldn't be who I am today without having had her in my life. I not only learned how to dance, perform, and always smile when walking into a room, I gained confidence. This woman was the epitome of what I mean when I say "unleash your sexy." Confidence. Power. Believing in yourself.

While of course I'm sad, I'm grateful. I'm grateful that I had the opportunity to be so close to a woman like her for so long. She is the meaning of inspiration, confidence, passion, and love. I thank her for being in my life and use what she taught us every day in my life and my work. I thank her for the friendships I will have for a lifetime. I thank her for my ability to dance any Greek dance on a whim.

As the priest said, do not copy others. Follow your own fervor. Use this incredible woman and the other inspirational people in your life as examples. Use what they taught you. Live your life with happiness, love, and confidence in you.

Today: What legacy do you want to be known for? What can you do today to create that?

SCHEDULE YOUR THOUGHTS

The moment when…

> You question everything.
> You feel like nothing you do is right.
> You feel like you can never get ahead.
> You feel like you just can't find the time.
> You're scared…of the unknown.
> You're mad…for not trying hard enough.
> You're sad…that you aren't as successful as someone else.
> You're nervous…about everything.

All of these thoughts and feelings are what make up stress and anxiousness. We're told constantly to combat stress to relax, but fighting stress isn't the solution.

Being aware, understanding, accepting, and releasing the feelings that are underneath the stress is what makes you feel better. Breathing deeply, relaxing your body, and calming your brain makes you feel better. Moving your body to let the feelings and energy flow through you makes you feel better. Reminding yourself that everything is okay right now in this moment makes you feel better.

Worrying can freeze us, unable to move, think, or make magic happen. But sometimes, even if you are breathing, doing yoga, and talking yourself out of your stress, it doesn't work. So I want to give you my secret for banishing worries in one minute. It's called scheduling your self-sabotaging thoughts. (Taken from my book, *Unleashed*, and adapted from a break-up article by Christine Hassler.)

Allot a certain amount of time per day (10 minutes) at a particular time (5pm) to think any negative thoughts you may be having right now. Yes, literally schedule your own thinking time. Whenever you start thinking these thoughts that aren't serving you and wasting your time during the day, remind yourself that you must wait until the time you've allocated to think them. Then continue on with your day.

Two things usually happen. Your allocated time arrives, you think about the thoughts you scheduled for 10 minutes, and you stop and move on. Or, time goes on throughout your day and completely forget what those thoughts even were.

The frustrations you have in life can be alleviated through thought management. If you can manage your thoughts, you'll have more time and you'll feel better about yourself. You are your thoughts, so when you push them out of your head, tell yourself to do your work, and schedule a time to think about how badly you feel about yourself later, you'll find that you'll end up feeling better about yourself because you actually did what you set out to do.

When you schedule time during the day to beat up on yourself and feel sorry for yourself, you'll realize it is a complete waste of time. Think about it, isn't it a bit ridiculous?

Today: Try scheduling your thoughts. Notice how much more productive you are.

FOCUS ON YOUR PRIORITIES

Overwhelm. We've all been overwhelmed. But what happens when you start using "overwhelm" as a noun instead of its intended verb usage?

Overwhelm as a noun starts organizing all things you consider overwhelming, stressful, or nerve-inducing into one bucket. And that bucket is the "overwhelm" in your life.

I have to deal with all of this overwhelm.
My stress and overwhelm are tearing me apart.

So how do you deal with this overwhelm? Thought management. If you manage your thoughts, you are able to manage your time. The key to managing your thoughts is identifying your priorities. If you're feeling overwhelmed, chances are you're also saying you have no time.

I have no time. = This is not a priority.

I find myself using the dreaded time excuse when I am thinking about things I want to do, but tell myself I have no time.

If you want something badly, then you'll do it. It doesn't even matter if you need it, if you truly want it, then you will do it.

When you tell yourself that you have no time to exercise, read a book, cook a fabulous dinner, or start your business…what you're really saying is that none of those things are priorities for you right now. Maybe they will be in the future, but not right now. You're also saying this because you feel overwhelmed and can't possibly think about adding in one more thing to your day.

Truthfully though, you do have this time. It's there. You just don't want to use it for those things you say you want to do. So, do you really want to do them? What's holding you back?

Start substituting "This isn't a priority for me" every time you say "I have no time." See what happens. Then break down your big tasks into smaller ones, like I break down my clients' goals into smaller, more manageable weekly goals.

If you are shaking your head saying this is easier said than done, let's do it together.

So, what if your big bucket of overwhelm is overflowing? How do you get out of it?

1. Acknowledge that you feel overwhelmed. Write about it. Talk to your friends. Vent. Let it out. Holding it in does no good.

2. Remember that you have the power to reduce the overwhelm. You have more control of the situations in your life than you think. Make a decision and stick with it. Often our stress and overwhelm stem from indecision.

3. Decide on one big task to work on and break it down into smaller tasks. As soon as you have a smaller task, do it. Just one. You will feel so much better that you started something. And the chance is high you will keep going.

Today: Write down your priorities. Make a list of five things you actually want to do. Pick one thing to work on this week and start doing it. If your priorities seem like monstrous tasks that overwhelm you, ask yourself if they really are priorities or if you can break them down into smaller chunks.

DOING NOTHING CAN BE PRODUCTIVE

The time to relax is when you don't have time for it.
— SYDNEY J. HARRIS

Ever notice that when you have the most to do, you want to do nothing? Your brain shuts down and your attention span only lasts about eight seconds. (According to 2015 statistics, the average attention span for a human is eight seconds. The average attention span for a goldfish is nine seconds. Yikes.)

Hopefully I caught your attention and you made it to this next line.

You put so much pressure on yourself to be a superhero at work and at home. To be a perfect parent, to be a supportive friend, to be a thoughtful significant other, to be the rockstar employee, to be the next top 40 under 40 entrepreneur, to nail that gig/job/spot/pitch/article…the list goes on. It's pretty darn exhausting.

You are doing the best you can do. But it's really important to take care of your mind and body.

Turn your phone off.
Take a nap.
Go for a walk.
Lay in the grass and look at the clouds. (Seriously when was the last time you did that?)

If none of that works, lay on the floor for two minutes. Put your legs up the wall if you want to get fancy. Simply get away from yourself.

Taking those two minutes gives you a rest from the constant stimulation. The phone scrolling, the laptop screen, your clients, your family, and even yourself. You know when the best ideas come to you—in the shower. Why? It's the only place you aren't distracted. You're in there for one mission. Why not replicate that elsewhere? The act of doing nothing and the act of focusing on one thing only (this is why in meditation they say to focus on your breath) give you the moments of clarity and focus you need.

I know what you're thinking—you will feel really guilty if you take time to do nothing because you have so much other stuff to do.

Put "do nothing" in your calendar. Schedule it. Do all the work, be the superhero, do whatever you have to do, but then take some time to do nothing. Your mind and body will thank you for it. I'm going for a walk right after I finish writing this.

Today: Schedule "do nothing" in your calendar for at least 10 minutes. Stick to your schedule.

STOP DOUBTING YOURSELF

"I have no experience. I can't charge that much." - a client said while talking about pricing her services.

"I'm scared to go to the new yoga studio. I'm intimidated that I'm not at the same level as anyone there." - a client said about starting up her yoga routine again.

"I can't go into that Zumba class. I'll look like a fool because everyone already knows the routine." - a client said when talking about classes she'd like to try.

"I'm terrible at running long distances. I've only run three miles and hated it." - me, a few years ago.

Wow, you can really be mean. Why don't you believe in yourself?

Here's my response to all of these pity parties:

"You do have experience. Ask for testimonials. And charge what you're worth. Don't worry about what others are charging." - Her services are sold out.

"Get yourself over to that yoga studio and sign up. Yoga is not about comparison games. There's a reason it's called a yoga *practice*." - She loved the new studio.

"There are new people in classes every day. Eventually you'll be the one who knows the routine. Tell the instructor you are new before class. And no one's looking at you anyway...they're checking out themselves in the mirror." - She had so much fun in class.

"You can run long distances if you really want to. Go slow. Don't time yourself. Don't compare yourself to others. Just get out there and do it." - I ran two 10K races and a half-marathon within one year after never running long distances.

It's totally normal to let these thoughts go through your head. But you'll never beat them if you believe them. You'll never do what you want if you believe them. And you sure as hell won't feel good if you believe them.

Stop showing up for the pity party you are throwing for yourself. You're so much better than that.

Today: What are you holding back on? Have a pity party for yourself. Look back at what you said to yourself and flip it around to work for you, not against you.

YOU ARE INCOMPARABLE

The comparison game is one that many can't escape. I consistently hear this from the people around me who are comparing their definitions of success: school grades, jobs, relationships, weddings, business growth, promotions, money. You name it, someone's comparing it. Social media makes it even worse as it highlights the "best of" someone's life, so naturally people assume that everyone around them is society's version of perfect—perfect gifts from spouses, perfect children, perfect jobs/businesses, perfect meals, perfect vacations, perfect friends—with perfectly staged photos highlighting all of this.

Comparing yourself to someone else is unreasonable. Is anyone in the world exactly the same as you? Your life is made up of your experiences. Everyone sees the world differently.

You are frustrated that you haven't seen the results you wanted yet, and someone else has. You feel down that you thought you'd be in a different place in your life at your age, and it feels like everyone else is farther ahead of you.

You want immediate results and instant satisfaction in a world that has centered itself on providing us with what we want faster than we ever thought we could get it.

You're looking to get ahead, fast. Thinking about next week, next month, or next year. But you're not thinking about today. You're not thinking about this week.

The only way to get immediate results is to focus on today. What you do today is who you are next week. You can become the person you want to be by putting in the work today.

Stop wasting time comparing yourself to others who seem to have done it faster or easier. Even the most successful will tell you it took them many years to become overnight successes.

Instead of comparing yourself to others, why not think of all the unique talents you have brought to your life, other people's lives, and the world? Why not appreciate the talents others have brought to you and the world as well?

Stop wasting your precious time and energy comparing yourself to others, thinking about others, wondering why it's taking you so long, and worrying that you'll never make it. That kind of thinking is creating your tomorrow. Is that what you want your tomorrow to be filled with?

Today: Are you comparing yourself to someone else? Use that energy to focus on you. Use today to get where you want to be tomorrow.

CREATE YOUR OWN MANTRA

Mantras are always there for you.

Feeling nervous? There's a mantra for that. Feeling sad? There's a mantra for that. Need to make a decision? A mantra will solve that.

As you read through each mantra in this book, it's likely you felt like I was talking directly to you about a situation presently occurring in your life. I often receive emails from readers saying, "Wow, are you in my head?" Many of us have parallel thoughts and feelings.

In addition to using the mantras in this book and online, you can also create a mantra for your specific situation.

Create as many as you want whenever you want. Mantras are here to guide you through your thoughts and feelings to uncover your true self. They can be situation specific, feelings specific, person specific—they can apply to anything that is happening in your life. I create mantras every day. Some stay with me for years, some are only needed for a particular event.

Get comfortable in a quiet setting. Breathe in through your nose and out through your mouth three times. Feel into your body. Ask yourself the following questions. Write down the answers on the following pages or in your notebook.

1. "How am I feeling right now?"

Think about your real feelings. Overwhelmed? Nervous? Scared? Angry? Really pay attention and be honest with yourself. What are you feeling in this moment?

2. "What am I thinking right now to make me feel this way?"

These are the thoughts that are making you feel how you responded in question one. Are you thinking specific things that are making you feel this way?

3. "How do I want to feel?"

Think about how you REALLY WANT to feel. When I do this exercise, my answers are usually: peaceful, calm, or happy.

4. "What thought could make me feel this way right now?"

What specific thought will help you start feeling the way you want to feel? This doesn't always come easily. Try to think of something that is true. If you feel like you aren't good enough at your job, your new thought would be, "I am good enough, I do excellent work." If you are very deep into your fears, this may take longer to pull out.

If you're feeling stuck, you can ask yourself, "What is the opposite of my fearful thought?" or "What would my best friend tell me right now if I told him/her how I was feeling?"

5. Create a mantra out of your new thought.

Take one thought (you may need to shorten it) and repeat it to yourself whenever you are feeling stressed, anxiety, or fearful again. Write it on a post-it, store it in your phone, or create a big photograph to hang up. This is your reminder to check-in with yourself about your thoughts and feelings. Are you harping on situations that aren't serving you? Use your mantra to snap back into your reality.

Sometimes you will exclaim a mantra immediately. You needed to be given the opportunity to say it aloud. You needed to create space to listen to your intuition.

Sometimes you have to ponder these questions a little longer. But don't ponder too long because that invites the thoughts to come back in. You are trying to access your right brain to listen to your intuition. Listen to whatever intuitive thoughts immediately enter your mind.

Don't over-think it. Let it flow. Trust yourself.

YOUR MANTRAS:

CONCLUSION

"What are your top three words for living in Paris now, one year later?"

This Parisian radio host did her homework. I was simultaneously shocked and impressed she found a blog post I wrote when I had moved to Paris one year earlier. The blog post referenced a tweet a girlfriend sent to me after living in Paris for ten days. "If you had three words to describe Paris so far, and you can only use magical once, what would they be?" My response: Charming, Indulgent, Natural.

Confession: I never prepare for interviews. I love the rush of spontaneity. Perhaps this is because I have a plan for nearly everything else in my life. Yes, I'm a planner. But I also believe that everything always works out. Maybe not the way you wanted or maybe more than you ever could have dreamed, but it works itself out somehow into what's supposed to happen for you. Plus, I know myself. I know my brand. I know my business. I know why I do this.

So when the radio host asked me that question, my brain raced through the last year of my life in Paris. I thought about the charming, movie-scene worthy streets I wandered, the massive monuments built thousands of years ago that I casually walked by on my way to meet friends, the quaint windows filled with roses and peonies, the perfectly manicured parks loaded with sunbathing chairs, sipping on rosé on the packed terraces, and the inspiring and welcoming group of expatriates that I've come to call my friends and colleagues.

I also thought about the ugliness I've encountered: people who weren't willing to help, always feeling like a foreigner no matter how comfortable I had become, being told it's not possible to do, get, or be what I want, nightmare administration and paperwork, endless negativity in work and life, and the wins and losses of learning a new language and culture with a less-than-welcoming nature.

"Natural, confused, and sunny." Those are the words that spewed out of my mouth when the radio host asked me the question about how I felt one year later.

The wide eyes of the radio host's face told me she surely wasn't expecting those answers, and neither was I. I couldn't believe those words came out. They certainly didn't sound as eloquent as I had hoped. How was I going to explain myself?

I still feel natural in Paris as it's an easy city to maneuver, but I'm always confused. Whether it's the direction I'm attempting to go in or trying to understand why things are done a certain way. Life seems easy here, until you realize that it's extremely complicated for no particular reason.

So if I'm always confused, why did I blurt out "sunny" as my final word?

I wasn't speaking literally. It rains *beaucoup* in Paris. But to live in this city, you have to keep the sun shining brightly inside of you at all times. If you do not have a sunny outlook on life while you live here, this city has no problem tearing you apart. Keep the sun's light inside of you and you will emerge stronger each and every time.

Why all this talk about Paris? Isn't Paris supposed to be the city of love and light with perfect women and to-die-for cuisine? As my friend Paul Angone says, "The grass is always greener on the other side, until you get there and realize it's because of all the manure."

The first time I visited Paris was for my 30th birthday, less than one year before I moved there. I had moved around America before but not abroad. It was always a fantasy of mine so when my then fiancé mentioned the prospect of moving to Paris for a career opportunity, a city I felt at home in with a language I studied in school, you'd think my immediate reaction would be sheer bliss. It wasn't. Fear and doubt overcame me.

For the first time in my adult life, I had started to feel established. My 20s were filled with studying marketing at a fashion school, working in three different advertising agencies in New York and San Diego, dating men completely the opposite of one another, completing my masters degree in 10 months in Washington D.C., and starting three businesses. At 30, I finally felt like I was doing what I loved, had found the love of my life, and was making a name for myself in New York. I was happy. I was building my reputation. And I was healthy again. So, was I willing to leave everything I built to start over, so new that I had to learn how to speak again?

Yes. But I was terrified.

Enter: the mantras. I created a mantra for every fear that ran through my mind and body because that ego voice whispering in my ear wasn't serving me at all. It was telling me that I wouldn't be able to eat anything because the French only eat cheese and cream. It was telling me I wouldn't make any friends. It was telling me I would lose all the progress I made in my life, business, and health. It was telling me I wouldn't make it.

When you move across the Atlantic Ocean in less than two months, to a country where you know no one, can't speak the language, need to continue to build your business, must gather all of the paperwork to apply for a visa, get married, meet with immigration, and then go through countless interviews to prove I'm legitimate. Oh and also plan a wedding back in the USA at the same time.

Enter: "You are stronger than you think you are." "Stop doubting yourself." "Enjoy the adventure, you will thrive."

When someone doesn't understand your accent or you don't understand their accent, you can't figure out what the ingredients are, get sent to four stores without addresses to buy a simple mason jar, you attempt a walk-in appointment but you get a look of disgust, the visa woman screams her face off at you, or your bus stops service for no reason when you're in a rush to get somewhere and you can't find the next bus stop.

Enter: "Find comfort in getting lost." "Center yourself." "Don't take it personally."

When fear of missing out leaves you in a puddle of tears. When you miss your friends' bridal showers, bachelorette parties, baby showers, birthday parties, and weddings. When all you want is to have a glass of champagne with your best friend on a terrace overlooking the Eiffel Tower. When your favorite people in the world are hurting or celebrating.

Enter: "Accept what you can't control." "Disappointment doesn't have to exist." "You are incomparable."

When you worry about no one showing up to your workout classes, creating coaching programs that will be successful, building trust with new friends and clients, losing your spark, finding motivation, adapting to the cultural differences, and being remembered.

Enter: "Believe." "Let it be easy." "Be kind to yourself."

When you want to appreciate the beauty around you, embrace the culture that baffles you, be aware of your growth and evolution, be thankful for meeting exotic inspiring people, respect yourself and others who are different from you, and be grateful for every positive or negative experience because it's making you a better person.

Enter: "Love where you live." "Live in your reality." "Know who you are."

I attended a networking group meeting the day after I arrived in Paris, freshly jet lagged yet ready to get started on my new life. I received a round of applause when I said I had been living in Paris for 24 hours and wide eyes and smiles abound when I said I help women unleash their sexy. That group subsequently named me the expat who transitioned the fastest to living in Paris and has since been a source of inspiration, motivation, and "home." And I had my mantras to thank for that.

Every time I'm scared, nervous, sad, or angry, I use a mantra to find myself again. I use all of the mantras in this book regularly. I create new mantras nearly every day based on what I'm feeling and what I'm experiencing. I refuse to let any other voice bring me down. I know myself. I believe in myself. I trust myself. When self-doubt creeps in, I don't let it win. I know I'm better than that. And I want you to know you're better than that too.

You are in control of how you are going to feel with each passing day, in each passing moment. You'll sometimes forget you have this control. Your fears, worries, and stress will sometimes get the best of you. But know you can turn yourself around. Know you have the power, and the remedy now, to transform your mindset and live your life truly unleashed.

Sanity is sexy and this book is your elixir.

BELIEVE MANTRAS

LET IT BE EASY

YOUR MINDSET CAN CREATE MIRACLES

KNOW WHO YOU ARE

YOU ARE THE OBSERVER OF YOUR THOUGHTS

ACT ON WHAT THE UNIVERSE PRESENTS TO YOU

ACCEPT WHAT YOU CAN'T CONTROL

BE KIND TO YOURSELF

LIVE IN YOUR REALITY

LOVE WHERE YOU LIVE

EXPANSION MANTRAS

ACCEPT OTHERS AS THEY ARE

FORGIVE FOR YOU

FEEL THE WAY YOU WANT TO FEEL

IT'S NOT YOUR PROBLEM

YOU CAN'T PROTECT OTHER PEOPLE'S FEELINGS

YOU DON'T HAVE TIME FOR THAT

SIDELINE THOSE WHO ARE RUINING YOUR GAME

DON'T LOWER YOUR STANDARDS

DISAPPOINTMENT DOESN'T HAVE TO EXIST

RELATIONSHIPS ARE NOT HARD

ATTRACT YOUR IDEAL RELATIONSHIP

SANITY IS SEXY

FIND FREEDOM MANTRAS

STOP CARING SO MUCH

RELEASE THE PATTERN

YOU CAN CONTROL THE OUTCOME

CHANGE IS GOOD

STOP SHOULDING

FIND COMFORT IN GETTING LOST

CENTER YOURSELF

CONQUER YOUR FEAR

FEEL INVINCIBLE MANTRAS

YOU CAN HAVE IT ALL

GIVE YOURSELF MORE CREDIT

YOU ARE STRONGER THAN YOU THINK YOU ARE

START NOW

FAILURE DOESN'T HAVE TO EXIST

PUSH PAST THE FEAR

CREATE YOUR LEGACY

SCHEDULE YOUR THOUGHTS

FOCUS ON YOUR PRIORITIES

DOING NOTHING CAN BE PRODUCTIVE

STOP DOUBTING YOURSELF

YOU ARE INCOMPARABLE

ACKNOWLEDGEMENTS

Thank you to the driven, passionate people in my life.

My parents always told my brother and I to do what we love. They ended up raising two entrepreneurial globetrotters. They're happy for us, though I believe they wish we would stop moving and settle somewhere. At least we're each married off. They remain our biggest supporters.

I love the way my husband loves me. He is always there for me no matter what, even after his exhausting days at work. He's truly my life partner. His incredible outlook on life and kind heart make me so grateful to have him.

My brother, Steven Antholis, designed this cover with two pieces of inspiration I gave him. It's exactly what I envisioned. He's designed my website graphics, helped me film workout videos on a hot, New Jersey beach, and showed me what it's like to be a backpacker. He's helped me grow more than he knows.

When you hire an editor and copywriter to help you with the finishing touches on the most important pieces of the book, you want it to be Megan Atkinson. She worked magic with my crazy deadline. And with the brainstorming involving Megan and Coach Jennie, the title of this book was born. Thank you.

My friends are my family. I am so grateful for the support and love. It keeps me going. I had many volunteers read this book before it was published to make sure it was of value to all of you. The feedback, the notes, the brainstorming, and the accountability will never be forgotten. A special thank you to Lauren, Arete, Catherine, and Jennifer for going above and beyond.

Thank you to my Paris community, online community, and coaches and mentors for helping me grow this business and writing career. You mean the world to me.

SANITY IS SEXY

ABOUT THE AUTHOR

Diana Antholis is an Author and Lifestyle Coach who empowers women to live unleashed; encouraging them to believe in themselves, expand their opportunities, find freedom, and feel invincible in their personal and professional lives.

Diana takes the mind, body, and soul approach to health and happiness in her globally-recognized Unleash Your Sexy Program. She works with her international clients to design lives they love; helping them to regain confidence, define work/life balance, implement self-care routines, and unleash their sexy selves, all while continuing to succeed in their careers and businesses. Her clients have gained a new perspective on their lives; feeling stronger, more balanced, and more in control. They have created booming businesses, been promoted, and developed better relationships. They have discovered how to live happy, healthy, fulfilling lives. They are living their lives unleashed.

As author of the bestselling books *Unleashed: Live the Balanced, Centered, and Sexy Life You Deserve* and *Sanity is Sexy: Mantras to Inspire a Healthy Mindset,* Diana pens manuals for women to live unleashed, sexy lives; empowering and providing them practical and actionable steps to find themselves again and release the fear and stress bringing them down.

Diana's background in corporate advertising, management and career consulting, and higher education led her to experience first-hand the immense stress occurring in the workplace and how it affects productivity, morale, and health. As she developed her own tools and resources to live a more balanced, centered, and sexy life, she realized she needed to help others navigate their own lives in such stressful environments. She found the secret: create your own happiness because no one else will do it for you.

Diana grew up in New Jersey, studied and worked in New York City, San Diego, Washington D.C., and currently lives in Paris, France. Diana's master's degree is in Organizational Management from The George Washington University in Washington D.C. Her bachelor's degree is in Advertising and Marketing Communications from the Fashion Institute of Technology in NYC. She holds certifications from the American Council on Exercise: Certified Personal Trainer, Certified Mind Body Specialist, and expert on alternative and integrative nutrition and women's nutrition for reproductive health.

When Diana isn't working with her clients, she can be found traveling, brewing her own kombucha, perfecting her chocolate chip cookie recipe, or doing yoga in the park. She continuously challenges herself in life and business while taking care to maintain her sanity on a daily basis. She wants women around the world to do the same: do what they love and live a luxurious life of ambition and leisure. Her coaching program, courses, books, and retreats can be accessed worldwide at DianaAntholis.com.

UNLEASH YOUR SEXY MANTRA

Sexy is when you feel good about you.
Your mind. Your body. Your being.

Sexy is enjoying life. Staying open. Staying centered.

Sexy is genuine happiness. When you smile because life is magnetic. When you appreciate the abundance in your life.

Sexy is when you stop worrying and over-thinking.
It's when you let it happen, when you let it flow.

Sexy is accepting that you are beautiful, strong, and capable.

Sexy is when you've made the ever-important decision to accept yourself—no matter what.

Unleashing your sexy is a mindset. It's being you.

If *Sanity is Sexy* has transformed the way you think, I'd love to hear from you. Write to me at diana@dianaantholis.com

Join the Unleash Your Sexy Community. It's free. You'll also receive a Monday Mantra every week in your inbox. DianaAntholis.com/membership

Connect with me online. I'm the only Diana Antholis in the world, which means I rank on the first page of Google.